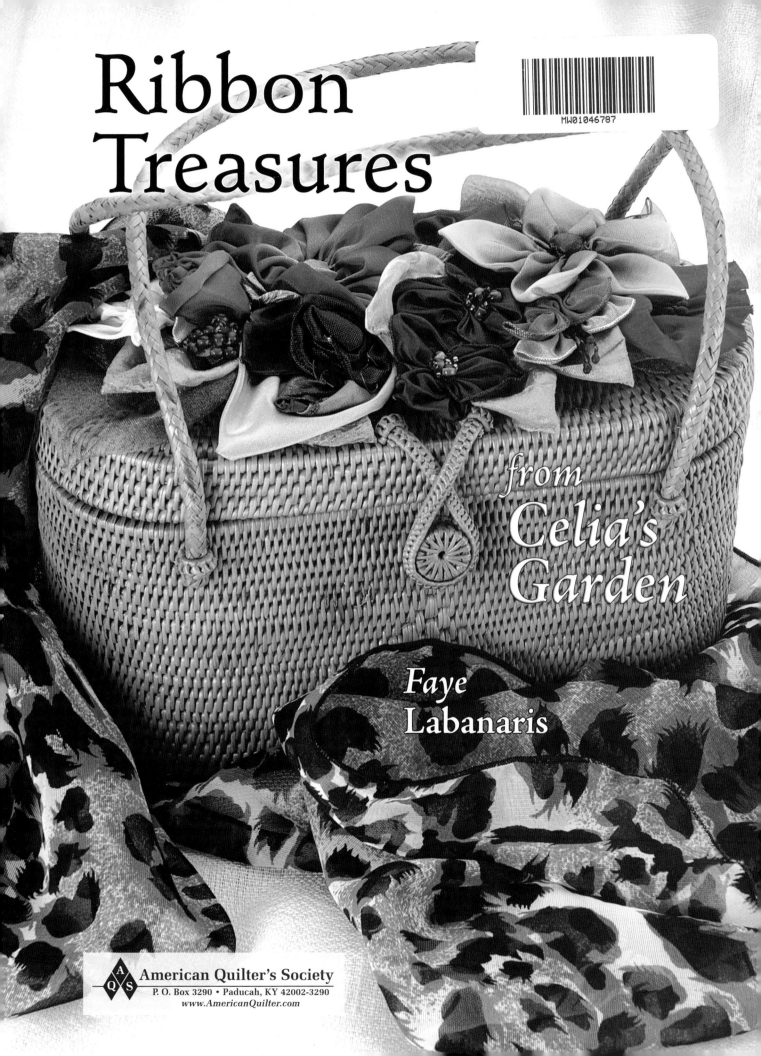

Ribbon
Treasures

from
Celia's
Garden

Faye
Labanaris

American Quilter's Society

P. O. Box 3290 • Paducah, KY 42002-3290

www.AmericanQuilter.com

MW01046787

Located in Paducah, Kentucky, the American Quilter's Society (AQS) is dedicated to promoting the accomplishments of today's quilters. Through its publications and events, AQS strives to honor today's quiltmakers and their work and to inspire future creativity and innovation in quiltmaking.

EXECUTIVE EDITOR: ANDI MILAM REYNOLDS
SENIOR EDITOR: LINDA BAXTER LASCO
GRAPHIC DESIGN: ELAINE WILSON
COVER DESIGN: MICHAEL BUCKINGHAM
PHOTOGRAPHY: CHARLES R. LYNCH, UNLESS OTHERWISE NOTED

P. O. Box 3290 • Paducah, KY 42002-3290
www.AmericanQuilter.com

Additional copies of this book may be ordered from the American Quilter's Society, PO Box 3290, Paducah, KY 42002-3290, or online at www.AmericanQuilter.com.

Library of Congress Cataloging-in-Publication Data

Labanaris, Faye.
Ribbon treasures from Celia's garden / by Faye Labanaris.
p. cm.
Includes bibliographical references.
ISBN 978-1-57432-958-2
1. Ribbon work. 2. Ribbon flowers. 3. Thaxter, Celia, 1835-1894. I. Title.

TT850.5.L32 2008
677'.76--dc22

2008031173

Proudly printed and bound in the United States of America

Dedication

To my family and friends, whose love and support are the most precious flowers in my garden.

To my students, whose enthusiasm for making ribbon flowers has resulted in this revised edition.

To Celia Thaxter, whose love of flowers has inspired the creation of blossoms for this book.

Acknowledgments

One person can make a quilt, but writing a book is a different story. It takes many people to ensure its arrival in the hands of the reader. As a seasoned author, I am still realizing just how much of a group effort it is to produce a book. To all those involved in the many stages of this book's production at the American Quilter's Society, I thank you very much for such a wonderful job!

Thank you to:

Meredith Schroeder, publisher and president of the American Quilter's Society for many years of publishing my books and your support throughout. It has been a pleasure to work with such a fine, professional, and personable company.

Andi Reynolds, executive editor, for bringing my ribbon dream book to perfection.

Nicole Chambers, former executive editor, for her vision to make my ideas into a beautiful ribbon book. She made me create beyond my expectations.

Linda Baxter Lasco, senior editor, for picking up the pieces. Thank you for working above and beyond in such a short time.

Barbara Smith, former executive editor on three of my books, for her superb editorial skills and patience, above and beyond, in dealing with all the concerns of an author. Her calmness, professionalism, and insight gave me much encouragement and support in times of doubt.

Elly Sienkiewicz, my teacher and my friend, for her Foreword for this book and her continued excitement and support from the first moments of this book.

Star Island Corporation and Vaughn Cottage/Thaxter Museum curators; Jane Vallier, author of *Poet on Demand,* for encouraging me to tell Celia's story through flowers; Peter Randall, photographer and publisher of Shoals-related materials; Special Collections librarians at Portsmouth Library, Portsmouth, New Hampshire; Miller Library, Colby College, Maine; Shoals Marine Lab, Cornell University, Ithaca, New York; University of New Hampshire Photography Department, Shoals Collections, Durham, New Hampshire.

Old friends and new, my students, guild members, people who have heard my lecture or seen Celia's quilt, thank you for your excitement and for your desire to hear more of her story.

My students for being so enthusiastic about making ribbon flowers and encouraging me to give instructions for more flowers. I hope you enjoy this book and have fun gardening with ribbon.

Quilter's Resource, Hannah Silk, and the Ribbon Studio for a lovely selection of ribbons to use in my ribbon palette for the creations in this book.

And thanks to my family for supporting me in what makes me happiest outside of my family. To my first born son, Andrew, for his drawings; to number two son, Tom, for his critique and quilt understanding; and to my husband, Nick, without whose care of the family and technical computer skills my books would not have been possible!

Faye Labanaris
MARCH 2008

Contents

Foreword

A number of summers ago, outside an Album Quilt class at the Vermont Quilt Festival, I met Faye Labanaris—a pretty, strong-minded woman with a spiritedness in her Mediterranean-dark eyes that caught my attention. In those years, Faye, a born teacher, was piloting an experimental science program for her local school district, while teaching quiltmaking on a regional scale and making prizewinning quilts. She did all this within the arms and obligations of a marriage blessed by a most supportive husband and two thriving sons. I didn't realize then that I would come to know Faye well.

In time, I would also learn that when Faye pronounces that you need to see something, you listen. A plain-spoken woman, she has perfected the art of verbal simplicity. I loved the three-line endorsement she gave on the back of my *Design a Baltimore Album Quilt* book. "Most necessary!" ran her entire first sentence. Now, here is Faye, telling us that there are quite wondrous things to be learned from a largely forgotten nineteenth-century poet, Celia Laighton Thaxter.

Like a quiltmaker's threaded legacy, Celia's poetry and prose left a tangible testament that speaks to us still. Through her written work, we can share her lyrical vision and the intimate kinship she felt with her corner of the world. Celia's expressive art may reveal something new about ourselves. Her Victorian life delivers a message for our modern times.

It intrigues me that Celia Thaxter created her art and won her fame along a path ever impeded by obstacles. Such a difficult life makes her an even more inspiring exemplar for us today. Life is never easy. Yet Celia chose, above all, to extol the beauty in her day-to-day existence and, by so doing, lived a life well worth examining.

Celia was known for her dauntless industry and compelling presence. Faye possesses these traits as well. Both exemplify a connection between a love of the flowering earth and a life of the mind that makes sense. How natural that we who come to quiltmaking with open hearts and minds anticipate hearing what Faye Labanaris can tell us about a kindred creative spirit: Celia Laighton Thaxter. Celia's message from the last century can help us ready ourselves to meet the future. What better protector, against the unknown, than the accumulated wisdom, the gathered blossoms, the virtuousness of this fine woman from the past? So, enter now the poetess Celia, with all thanks to the quiltmaker, Faye.

Elly Sienkiewicz
WASHINGTON, D.C. APRIL 1995

Celia Thaxter

Celia's Story

Photos used in Celia's Story are from the NH Collection Photographic Services, University of New Hampshire, unless otherwise noted.

I first met Celia in her garden. It was through her love of flowers that I got to know this remarkable and memorable woman. Born in Portsmouth, New Hampshire, in 1835, Celia Thaxter became one of America's first women authors and by the late nineteenth century she was probably its best known female poet and naturalist writer. Her last book, *An Island Garden,* was published just before her death in 1894 and is still available today and still widely read as a gardening classic.

White Island lighthouse and cottage

PHOTO: Peter Randall, Portsmouth. NH

Celia's father, Thomas Laighton, was a lighthouse keeper for White Island on the Isles of Shoals, a group of eight small rocky and almost barren islands that lie 10 miles off the New Hampshire coast. Thomas purchased four of the Isles of Shoals in 1835. He hoped to reestablish the once prosperous and profitable fishing industry on the Isles of Shoals.

Celia's years on White Island proved to be among the happiest in her life. The island was large enough for only the lighthouse and a cottage. Flowers were scarce and Celia treasured every one she saw. Her first garden was planted her first spring on White Island when she was five years old: *"I had a scrap of garden, literally not more than a yard square, wherein grew only African marigolds rich in color as barbaric gold."*[1] Her love of nature would never leave Celia, who wondered in awe how *"every flower knew what to do and to be."*[2]

Survival on the island drew the family together and gave them an inner strength that would sustain them the rest of their lives. Though Celia's father was happy as the keeper of White Island light, he had not completely given up his interests on the mainland. When he was elected to the Board of Selectmen in Portsmouth in 1841, his family moved into the Haley House on Smuttynose Island, which allowed him to commute by boat to the mainland. Subsequently, Thomas decided to dust off the sign on Captain Haley's old hotel and become an innkeeper. He then went on to build a grand hotel on nearby Appledore Island.

The Appledore House opened in 1848 and was the first resort on the eastern seaboard. In the summer of 1851 Celia became engaged to Levi. The hotel had just opened for the season, and guests were arriving daily including many of Levi's friends from Boston. They spent many happy hours in his cottage reading the poetry of Tennyson, Browning, Emerson, Longfellow, Hawthorne, and Whittier, reading their own verses, listening to music, and discussing social issues. Celia was very much a part of this very stimulating scene and would continue this tradition of conversation and readings later, with gatherings of authors and musicians in her own parlor on the island.

Appledore House and its dining room

Many famous guests included such artists, musicians, and writers as Thomas Bailey Aldrich, Henry Ward Beecher, Samuel Clemens, Richard Henry Dana, Childe Hassam, Nathaniel Hawthorne, William Morris Hunt, Samuel Longfellow, James Russell Lowell, Harriet Beecher Stowe, Sarah Orne Jewett, Lucy Larcom, James and Annie Fields, John Greenleaf Whittier, and Frances H. Burnett (whose *Little Lord Fauntleroy* was inspired by Celia's brother Cedric). Initially such notable people came to the Shoals because of Levi and Thomas, but in later years, they came to visit with the poet Celia.

Because the Appledore House was nearly self-sufficient, its operation involved a great deal of hard work for the Laighton family. At its peak, the hotel slept 500 guests and fed 900 at its tables. The hotel required a lot of Celia's physical strength and energy. Except for a few years early in her marriage, she spent every summer of her life out on the islands helping with the hotel.

Levi Lincoln Thaxter arrived on the Isles of Shoals in 1846. He was charmed by the islands and impressed with Thomas Laighton's ambitious dream of developing the islands as a summer resort. Levi enthusiastically joined Thomas in his venture to build a new hotel on Appledore Island and was hired to tutor the children. Celia was in awe of Levi's worldliness and his vast knowledge of poetry and literature. He soon recognized that Celia possessed unusual intellect and introduced her to a new world of contemporary poets.

An engaged Celia, age 15.   Levi at time of their marrige.

Levi's photo – Special Collections: Miller Library, Colby College, Waterville, ME

Celia was married to Levi in 1851 when she was 16 years old. The early years of their marriage were happy ones. Each evening Levi read poetry to Celia by the fireside and played music on their piano. This relaxed her and inspired her to write her own verses. In an 1857 letter she wrote, *"Such good evenings as we have! And they are so fascinating sometimes we don't break up the meeting till past eleven, never till after ten. We draw the table up to the roaring fire, and I take my work, and Levi reads to me."* [3]

Unfortunately, this happy scene was to change. Levi was not the hard worker that Celia's parents had been. By 1858, he had all but given up trying to find a job and became a gentleman of leisure. Levi's father purchased a "modest mansion" for the Thaxters in Newtonville, Massachusetts. Celia found herself caring for three small children, her husband, and a huge ark of a house with no household help.

Homesick for her family, Celia wrote many letters to them and would often send along the verses she composed in her head as she worked. One day a poem came to Celia as she was kneading bread in her Newtonville kitchen. She wrote it down on a piece of grocery paper. Without Celia's knowledge, this poem was sent anonymously by a friend to James Russell Lowell, the editor of *The Atlantic Monthly*. Lowell published "Landlocked" in the March 18, 1861, issue. Celia could hardly believe her eyes when she read her poem for the first time in the popular magazine and received a check for its publication. It was one of the happiest moments in her life.

Celia was an instant success. Other magazines wanted her verses. With fireside poetry the rage in America, she found that she could make money from the publication of her poems and submitted several each month to various publications, receiving $10 apiece. Celia had financial security for the first time in her married life. She hired help for chores and purchased a sewing machine for making shirts and patching trousers.

O happy river, could I follow thee!
O yearning heart, that never can be still!
O wistful eyes that watch the steadfast hill,
Longing for the level line of solemn sea!
THE POEMS OF CEILA THAXTER, "LANDLOCKED"

Celia's parent's cottage which became hers after their death

The many demands on Celia's time forced her to write most of her poetry in a state of physical, mental, and emotional exhaustion. As it became apparent that her eldest son Karl had developmental problems, Levi withdrew and spent his time with their second and third sons, John and Roland. Celia was left alone much of the time but found solace in the many letters she wrote to her friends. As she became more successful with her poetry publications, Levi and Celia's lives drifted further apart. Celia spent her summers on Appledore helping her family with the running of the hotel while Levi left the islands for good.

Celia's brothers, Oscar and Cedric, built a cottage for their parents near the hotel. Thomas died in 1866 not knowing the important role his daughter Celia would have in the "making of the Shoals." After Eliza died in 1877, Celia wrote many poems in her mother's memory. She moved into her parents' cottage on Appledore and tended Eliza's beautiful garden as a memorial to her. The cottage became known as the Thaxter Cottage and Celia began inviting talented guests for afternoons of music, poetry, and conversation.

Celia's mother, Eliza Rymes Laughton

Celia's Parlor

The success of Celia's poetry quickly earned her a place in Boston's intellectual and literary society. James T. Fields, her editor and publisher, and his young wife Annie took Celia under their wing and became her most intimate friends and counselors. She was devoted to them and they had a tremendous influence on her, both socially and professionally. Annie became Celia's confidant, as the poet poured out her heart in letters written over the years.

In the summer, her friends followed her to the Shoals, where each day she invited into her cottage parlor authors, artists, and musicians who had come to the islands for rest and

Celia with artists and musicians in the doorway of her cottage

Celia's parlor and her piazza with its chickenwire framework filled with flowers

inspiration. The atmosphere was stimulating, the music heavenly, and the flowers colorful and aromatic. Her parlor became a salon in the true sense of the word and served as a model for American summer art colonies.

Celia's Garden

"This is what I enjoy! To wear my old clothes every day, grub in the ground, dig dandelions, and eat them too, plant my seeds, and watch them grow."[4]

With fewer responsibilities after her mother's death, Celia was able to spend many delightful days in her island garden where her flowers were her only concern. She nurtured them. She studied them with a scientist's scrutiny. She loved them and they responded, blooming beautifully as they did for no other. She wrote, *"I feel the personality of each flower, and I find myself greeting them as if they were human. They stand in their peace and purity and lift themselves to my adoring gaze as if they knew my worship—so calm, so sweet, so delicate and radiant, I lose myself in the tranquility of their happiness."*[5]

Celia's was an old-fashioned garden, similar to one her grandmother might have planted. She chose flowers for their color, fragrance, and textures. Poppies, sweet peas, and roses were among her favorites. It was a picking garden and the moment of glory came when the flowers were in Celia's hand. She arranged her flowers *"almost as one would paint a picture, or compose a sonata."*[6]. Celia's garden inspired her artistic endeavors—flower arranging, china painting, and painting watercolor illustrations for books of poetry. She often awoke at dawn and soon was out with her flowers, tending them with such love that they had no choice but to bloom beautifully. She loved the process of gardening, to feel the earth in her hands, to marvel at the miracle of a seed sprouting into a beautiful creation. Even the tools she used were sacred in her hands.

The Winter of Celia's Life

The winter of 1877 was the last Celia was to spend on the island. She spent most of her winters in Portsmouth, New Hampshire. Painting flowers on china provided her with sufficient income to keep her comfortable during her last years. She would plant seedlings to prepare for

Photo of drawing of Celia at her painting table

her summer garden. *"When the snow is still blowing against the window-pane in January and February, and the wild winds are howling without, what pleasure it is to plan for the summer that is to be!"*[7]

Year after year, visitors came out to Appledore to see Celia's garden and marvel at her beautiful flowers. They would try to garden as she did in their own plots on the mainland, but to no avail. They would return to Celia and ask the secrets of her beautiful garden. Sarah Orne Jewett, one of Celia's dearest friends and an author herself, offered to give Celia the assistance she needed to write a garden book. With Sarah's encouragement and help *An Island Garden* was published in 1894.

Much more than a how-to-garden manual, *An Island Garden* tells of Celia's love affair with her island garden and the flowers she lovingly planted each year. She describes the personality and beauty of each flower and the seasonal changes that take place in a garden. Childe Hassam, America's foremost impressionist painter in the late nineteenth century, vacationed on Appledore and was fascinated by Celia's garden and parlor. He painted these special places hundreds of times and some of his finest works were included in *An Island Garden.*

A Poet's Burial

"When I saw Celia lying there the thought came to me that surely anyone so gifted and so beloved could not be lost forever."[8]

Celia was feeling poorly on August 25, 1894. She seemed to rally with the presence of her sons and their families, spending a happy day with them, reading some of her poems and enjoying her grandchildren. When she retired for the evening, she asked Minna, her beloved servant, to raise the curtains so she could see the morning light. Minna turned to Celia after opening the curtains, but in an istant she was gone. She had died suddenly at the age of 59.

Celia's two dearest friends, Annie Fields and Sarah Orne Jewett, recorded her passing with such poignant words that it is only appropriate to end this tribute with their reminiscences. Sarah Orne Jewett relates: *"Those who have known through her writings alone the islands she loved so much, may care to know how, just before she died, she paid, as if with dim foreboding, a last visit to the old familiar places of the tiny world that was so dear to her. Day after day she called those who were with her to walk or sail. Under the very rocks and gray ledges, to the far nests of the wild sea birds, her love and knowledge seemed to go. She was made of that very dust... but it seemed as if a little stardust must have mixed with the ordinary dust of those coasts; there was something bright in her spirit that will forever shine."*[9]

Her friend Annie Fields relates: *"And so, indeed, Celia Thaxter slipped away from those who loved her, leaving suddenly this beautiful, sorrowful world, wherein she had loved and rejoiced and sorrowed with the children of men. No letters, no records, no description, can express adequately the richness and tenderness of her nature; but in a vanishing of her large vitality she has drawn many a heart after her to scan more closely than ever before the slight veil swaying between the seen and the unseen."* [10]

After Celia's burial beside her parents, family and friends returned to her parlor. For over two hours they sat and listened to William Mason play the music Celia loved to hear. Her parlor was filled with her flowers, arranged by Appleton Brown and Childe and Maud Hassam, who knew how Celia would have wished everything organized.

Cedric Laighton   Oscar Laighton

Cedric and Oscar struggled to keep Appledore House running smoothly, but with Celia's passing, a major part of the charm of Appledore was gone forever. Cedric and his family moved into Celia's cottage where they continued to care for her garden and parlor, but they were not blessed with her love and devotion. Some time after Cedric's death, Appledore and Star Island were purchased by the Star Island Corporation for their summer conferences. Oscar remained welcome on Star Island where he had a home until he died at the age of ninety-nine years and nine months.

One day in September 1914, after Appledore House had closed for the season, a fire began and the 60-year old hotel quickly went up in flames. Winds spread the fire to nearby cottages. Oscar barely had time to get to his sister's cottage and rescue a few of her possessions before it, too, was engulfed in flames. Memories of the grand hotel were all that remained after the flames died down.

Appledore Island was abandoned after the fire and Celia's garden was overrun by brambles and poison ivy. It remained this way until the 1970s when the University of New Hampshire and Cornell University leased Appledore Island for the Shoals Marine Laboratory. In 1977, Dr. John Kingsbury, director of the Shoals Marine Lab, discovered the remains of Celia's cottage while surveying the island. Using the garden posts found in front of the cottage foundations and Celia's garden plan as presented in her book, he was able to resurrect the garden.

As head gardener, Virginia Chislom of Rye, New Hampshire, lovingly tended Celia's plants from the time the garden was first replanted. Her work is now carried on by the Rye Garden Club. In an effort supported by the University of New Hampshire, plants are transported out to the island each spring on the *M/V Thomas B. Laighton*. Visitors to the island can see Celia's garden and enjoy her flowers today just as she did over 100 years ago. You can also enjoy the flowers Celia loved by re-creating them with beautiful ribbons as described here in *Ribbon Treasures from Celia's Garden*.

My Garden

It blossomed by the summer sea,
A tiny space of tangled bloom
Wherein so many flowers found room,
A miracle it seemed to be!

Up from the ground, alert and bright,
The pansies laughed in gold and jet,
Purple and pied, and mignonette
Breathed like a spirit of delight.

Flaming the rich nasturtiums ran
Along the fence, and marigolds
"Opened afresh their starry folds"
In beauty as the day began,

While ranks of scarlet poppies gay
Waved when the soft south-wind did blow,
Superb in sunshine, to and fro,
Like soldiers proud in brave array.

And tall blue larkspur waved its spikes
Against the sea's deep violet,
That every breeze makes deeper yet
With splendid azure where it strikes;

And rosy-pale sweet-peas climbed up,
And phloxes spread their colors fine,
Pink, white, and purple, red as wine,
And fire burned in the escholtzia's cup.

More dear to me than words can tell
Was every cup and spray and leaf,
Too perfect for a life so brief
Seemed every star and bud and bell.

And many a maiden, fairer yet,
Came smiling to my garden gay,

Whose graceful head I decked always
With pansy and with mignonette.

Such slender shapes of girlhood young
Haunted that little blooming space,
Each with a more delightful face
Than any flower that ever sprung!

O shadowy shapes of youthful bloom!
How fair the sweet procession glides
Down memory's swift and silent tides,
Till lost in doubtful mists of gloom!

Year after year new flowers unfold,
Year after year fresh maidens fair,
Scenting their perfume on the air,
Follow and find their red and gold.

And while for them the poppies blaze
I gather, brightening into mine
The eyes of vanished beauty shine,
That gladdened long-lost summer days.

Where are they all who wide have ranged?
Where are the flowers of other years?
What ear the wistful question hears?
Ah, some are dead and all are changed.

And still the constant earth renews
Her treasured splendor, still unfold
Petals of purple and of gold
Beneath the sunshine and the dews.

But for her human children dear
Whom she has folded to her breast,
No beauty wakes them from their rest,
Nor change they with the changing year.

THE POEMS OF CEILA THAXTER, "MY GARDEN"

Beautiful Ribbon
How do I love thee? Let me count the ways!

I was first introduced to making flowers from ribbon by Elly Sienkiewicz in the early 1990s. She generously designed a wreath for a class I was to teach at a Maine quilt conference. The wreath had dimensional rosebuds made of beautiful French wire-edged ribbon. Making the rosebuds from this lovely ribbon was an unfamiliar technique for me and I was quickly captivated by this new medium and began using it in my appliqué designs. My garden of ribbon flowers has bloomed profusely since those first rosebuds.

Flowers make us happy. No matter if they are just in photographs, a small bud in a vase, or a garden full of blossoms. While we cannot all have beautiful gardens, we all do appreciate the beauty of flowers. There is something peaceful about working in a garden or even just arranging flowers in a vase or a bouquet.

Working with your hands and watching something grow from a seed or small plant into a thing of beauty is a satisfying experience. The same can be said when working with fabric or ribbon and creating something beautiful. You can have flowers year-round using ribbons to create lovely blossoms for your quilts, garments, or decorative items.

Ribbon has always been tied to our lives, from beautifully wrapped presents at Christmas and birthdays to award ribbons on our quilts. As children we were dressed for special occasions with a pretty ribbon in our hair or around our waist. Ribbons are beautiful and intriguing. They are something to be saved after the package is opened.

Working with ribbons and creating something other than bows has been a practice and art form for over 100 years. I enjoy working with ribbon as the flowers seem more realistic than when made with fabric. The dimensional look and texture of ribbonwork in my appliqué adds another level of interest to each piece.

Wire-edged ribbon was first manufactured during the nineteenth century in the Southern Lyon/Midi region of France. It was used to make floral embellishments for ladies' garments and fashion accessories. It was also used, as ribbon is traditionally used, to tie packages. In French confectionery shops, even today, the ribbon is used to tie purchases of sweets into beautiful presentations.

Originally made of silk, today's wire-edged ribbon is made of rayon and is colorfast. In addition to manufacturers in France, factories in Germany, Switzerland, and the United States now make a wide range of colors in both solid and variegated shades. These ribbons are as much a feast for the eyes as the delicious French confections are for the palate.

Today's high quality wire-edged ribbon has a thin copper wire along the selvage edge that will not rust. Beware of inexpensive wire-edged craft ribbon not made with copper wire. Less expensive metals may rust. Check the make-up of your ribbon by pulling back a tiny portion of the fabric covering the wire to check the type of wire used in the ribbon.

Wire-edged ribbon comes in many colors, textures, weights, and widths. Ribbon can make beautiful flowers that look realistic or creatively impressionistic. Each individual flower reflects the personality of its maker. It is impossible to fail when making ribbon flowers. Wire-edged ribbon flowers almost make themselves. You can also use regular unwired ribbon to fashion flowers and leaves with a softer look.

The techniques are simple and more economical than you might expect. Many flowers can be made with less than 12 inches of ribbon. Whenever I teach these flower-making techniques, my students can hardly wait for the introductory instructions to finish so they can begin making their first blossoms.

Enjoy creating the blossoms inspired by Celia's garden. I'll share my garden of ribbon flowers with you and hope that you, too, come to love this wonderful experience of gardening with ribbon.

Getting Started

Supplies

Scissors (three types):
    fabric scissors with 4"–6" blades
    embroidery scissors with sharp cut-to-the point tips
    utility scissors for cutting wire ribbon

Needles: milliners needles, sizes 9 and 10
    These are 1½" long. They are thin and sharp and perfect for work with ribbon. They can also be used as beading needles.

Pins: long thin, flower head pins; long silk pins

Thread: quilting thread or strong sewing thread; nylon beading thread
    Use a double strand of sewing thread or a single strand of the nylon beading thread. Do not use silk thread for stitching ribbon flowers as it is not strong enough.
    Use neutral thread to make the flowers and matching thread to anchor them.

Ruler: 12" or a tape measure

Crinoline: lightweight stabilizer for layering flowers
    Its cousin, buckram, is a heavyweight stiffener used for hat making and is too stiff to needle through. If you can't find crinoline in the bridal department of a fabric shop, use a lightweight interfacing that has some body and can be needled through. As an alternative, use a few layers of netting.

Hemostats or tweezers: grapping tools for working with wire-edged ribbon

Hair clips: short and long varieties
    These act as extra fingers to hold your work.

Beads: assorted sizes and colors
    Use these for flower centers; the yellows and golden browns are especially useful.

Stamens: Can usually be purchased from ribbon suppliers. Adding them to the center of the ribbon flowers gives them a more realistic look.

Embroidery floss: shades of yellow and golden brown
   Use for flower centers.

Trims: green and browns
   Use for leaves and stems.

Variety of ribbons: In various sizes—#3 (¾"), #5 (1"), and #9 (1½")—and of different types—French wire-edged ribbon, unwired satin, Hannah bias silk, velvet, jacquard, and picot edge ribbons to name a few.

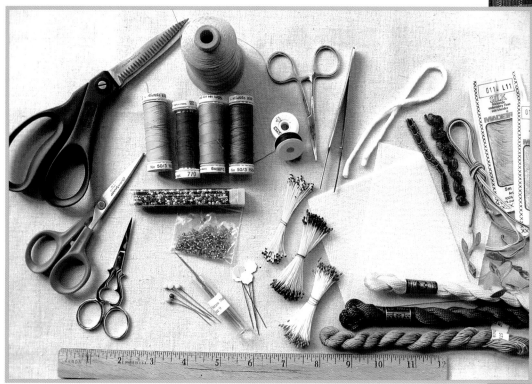

PHOTO: Faye Labanaris

Working with Ribbon

When making these flowers, use a double strand of quilting thread or a single strand of nylon beading thread. You need the thread strength because much of the flower's construction involves gathering and pulling. Start with a tiny knot and anchor it to the ribbon with a backstitch or two. Test with a gentle tug. Your knot should not slip through the ribbon. The stitch length should be a bit longer than when you are stitching fabric. The longer the stitch, the more pleats result and the smaller the opening of gathered ribbon centers. The smaller the stitches result in more gathers in the ribbon and larger gathered ribbon centers. You can, of course, adjust your stitch length to please yourself.

Be sure to pull up the gathers every few inches. This gather-as-you-sew process prevents the thread from twisting and breaking. Most of the time the color of the thread does not show between the gathers of the ribbon. A neutral color is a good choice. Thread matching the ribbon color is only needed when attaching the flower to your project.

Wire-Edged Ribbon

An advantage of wire ribbon is that it can be gathered without needle and thread. Push down on the cut edge of the ribbon to expose a tiny bit of the wire on one end of one side. Hold on to this wire with a grabbing tool, such as a hemostat or a pair of tweezers. Hold the wire and slide about ½" to 1" of ribbon down the wire. Bend the wire over the ribbon to prevent it from sliding back onto the wire. Repeat on the opposite end. Now you are ready to hold the wire and push the ribbon down to the center of the length, gathering equally from both ends.

It's easier to gather into the middle from each end rather than from one end to the other. There's less chance of wire breakage. Be careful not to pull the wire away from the ribbon at an angle. The razor-sharp wire can cut right through the ribbon, resulting in a frayed edge. If that happens, stop and secure the ribbon fray by wrapping the wire around the portion connected to the unexposed wired edge. Do not rush the process or pull too hard as the wire may break.

If the wire breaks, it is not the end of your flower. Try to recover the wire ends by poking them out through the edges of the ribbon and pushing the ribbon away from the wire so you will have enough wire to wrap around a bit of the ribbon to secure it. You may have to resort to needle and thread and hand stitch the remaining unwired portion of ribbon.

Working with Crinoline

In ribbonwork, the flower petals are arranged on a crinoline base. The flower is completely formed and tacked down with many stitches. The stitches are hidden through the many folds of ribbon. You can arrange the flower petals to your liking with these stitches. Do not make any stitches on the outer edge of the petals. They'll interfere with trimming the crinoline away from the finished blossom.

When the flower is complete, the excess unstitched crinoline is trimmed away from underneath the flower. Attach the flower to a quilt or garment with a few stitches through the crinoline base. Anchor the outer edges with thread that matches the flower.

Washing Ribbonwork

Sometimes a piece becomes soiled and can only be cleaned by washing. Try spot cleaning before you soak the entire piece. The ribbon is usually colorfast, but check first with a scrap of ribbon in a glass of cold to room temperature water. Soak the soiled piece in cold water with a very mild soap. Do not squeeze, but simply push gently up and down in the water. Keep rinsing the same way and gently press dry on a towel and air dry. The agitation of the washing machine and high temperature of a drier will harm your ribbonwork piece.

If pieces of loose ribbon become soiled, they can be washed in the same manner. The dried wrinkled ribbon can be ironed flat and be like new again. Use a setting on your iron for synthetics.

Storing Ribbon

It's fun to collect lots of wonderful types of ribbon. Keeping them neat and tidy and ready for future use can be a problem. Some people roll them around an empty paper towel tube. I find this method cumbersome. If you buy ribbon by the roll, just store the full roll on a shelf. My favorite method for odd lengths of ribbon is to wrap them around cardboard about 4" x 6" size. I sometimes use several thicknesses of large index cards as wrapping cards. I am able to get several varieties of ribbon on one card by wrapping the ribbon around the narrow width of the card. I can then store these ribbon cards in a plastic storage drawer container. When the drawer is open I can readily see the types of ribbons I have.

PHOTO: Faye Labanaris

Making Ribbon Flowers

Flowers can be broken down into individual petals, flower centers, buds, stems, and leaves. These components can be varied by changing the amount of ribbon you use to create them.

Ribbon blooms give a dimensional look that can be controlled by stitching them completely in place. The dimensional look is appropriate when used as a decorative element. Press ribbon flowers flat and use them for appliqué.

Don't be afraid to experiment by varying your stitching pattern or the length or width of the ribbon used. That's how new flowers are formed. The secret is not to cut the ribbon before you are sure you like the result. Stitch a sample, then decide. If you don't like it, just take the stitches out and start again. Have a notebook, pencil, and ruler handy to write down what you did. Note the length and width of the ribbon you used.

Just about every method of manipulating ribbon can be used to make flowers—folding, rolling, knotting, scrunching, gathering, stitching, thumb-twisting, pleating, or pinning. Leaves and petals are formed by any one of these techniques.

The length of your hand stitching will affect the end result. The longer the stitch, the more the ribbon will form pleats and create a tighter gather. The smaller the stitch, you'll have softer gathers and more ribbon on the thread. An average of 1–2 stitches to the quarter inch will get you nice results. You can, of course, adjust your stitch length to please yourself. You can vary the position of a straight running stitch from close to the ribbon's selvage edge to the center of the ribbon.

A quartet of mini clay flower pots bloom with an assortment of mini ribbon flowers.

Project Gallery

Sometimes you just need to relax and have some fun making a quick project with beautiful ribbons. The inspiration for these ribbon treasures came from the flowers Celia Thaxter grew in her beloved garden. They have been created for people who enjoy working with their hands and creating flowers with ribbon.

A black envelope purse enhanced with an edging of ribbon tent leaves and accented with a pin becomes a beautiful fashion accessory you'll enjoy using or giving as a gift. This example was a purchased bag, but a simple lined fabric envelope can easily be made.

A 3" length of satin taffeta 1½" wide (#9) wire-edged ribbon was used to make the tent leaves (page 79). The petals were arranged and anchored in place on a crinoline strip, then attached to the purse.

TOP LEFT: Let a circlet of daisies crown your Queen of the May or flower girl. Braid three lengths of 1" satin ribbon to form a crown. Make 6–8 daisies (page 48) from a variety of #9 ribbons with 5–6 petals per flower. Vary the centers of each daisy and attach at intervals around the crown. Tie 4" lengths of green satin ribbon on either side of the flowers for a leafy effect. Add a bow and tails of satin ribbon to trail down in the back.

BELOW LEFT: An heirloom pin is nestled in a cluster of tent leaves (page 79).

BELOW: For a keepsake wedding bouquet, make gathered roses (page 64) with an assortment of white and ivory ribbons—wire-edged, unwired, and silk. Faye's signature rose (pages 73–74) and six roses surround a center rose. For a domed effect, make an additional rose and fasten it on top of the center rose. Wide sheer ribbon of gathered leaves (page 83) and stems of Hannah silk cording (page 87) knotted at the end complete the bouquet.

"As I hold the flower in my hand and think of trying to describe it, I realize how poor a creature I am, how impotent are words in the presence of such perfection."

CELIA THAXTER, *AN ISLAND GARDEN*, P. 76

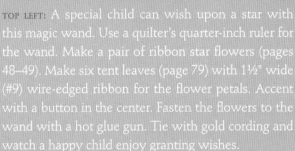

TOP LEFT: A special child can wish upon a star with this magic wand. Use a quilter's quarter-inch ruler for the wand. Make a pair of ribbon star flowers (pages 48–49). Make six tent leaves (page 79) with 1½" wide (#9) wire-edged ribbon for the flower petals. Accent with a button in the center. Fasten the flowers to the wand with a hot glue gun. Tie with gold cording and watch a happy child enjoy granting wishes.

TOP RIGHT: Tie up a sachet of fragrant potpourri in a square of sheer fabric and tie with a decorative cord and sheer ribbon in a matching color. Accent with a lace doily and a generously sized flower made with plaid ribbon. The rose is made with 1 yard of 1½" wide (#9) plaid ribbon. Twist the last half of the gathers into 3 petals. The outer row of petals is made with 6" of 1½" wide (#9) ribbon, folded and formed into pinch-pleat petals. Make 5 petals and attach at the base of the rose, then fold them so they curve up and outward for a lovely effect.

BOTTOM RIGHT: This lovely little satin and brocade journal is accented with a trio of beautiful picot-edged velvet leaves (page 80), double layer rosebuds (page 76), and simple gathered rose (page 64), tapestry ribbon and pearls. A ribbon bookmark extends beyond the notebook and is enhanced with tails of beads.

LEFT: A wide yellow grosgrain ribbon encircles a straw hat with a triple flat bow. A wreath of gathered leaves (page 83) made from 1½" wide (#9) checkered ribbon forms the basis for a collection of different flowers made from the same yellow green plaid ribbon—loosely gathered roses (page 64), five petal posies (page 32), and pointy petal flowers (page 48)—all tied together with a length of green Hannah silk cording. The centers are accented with golden beads.

BELOW LEFT: A green straw summer tote bag is the perfect spot for a cluster of yellow round petal flowers (page 55), daisies (pages 48–49), and a golden sunflower (pages 48–49). Fill with a bouquet of assorted flowers.

BELOW: A purchased denim tote bag becomes a matching fashion accessory when embellished with the same black grosgrain tent leaves as the jacket (page 27). Use a strip of crinoline for the mounting base in the length desired. Arrange the petals on the crinoline, then stitch onto the tote bag. The bag's quilted cross-hatch stitching is embellished with a black bead at the intersections. To complete the customized look, the zipper pull has a leafy beaded fob.

Ribbon Treasures from Celia's Garden ❀ Faye Labanaris

TOP LEFT: Soft tent leaves (page 79) and a beaded center flower enhance this eyeglass case.

TOP RIGHT: A denim jacket becomes a one-of-a-kind original with embellishments of tent leaves (page 79) made from ½" wide (#9) black grosgrain, accented with 4 mm black pearl beads. Use 3" of ribbon per petal and mount on crinoline cut to match the curved shape and length of the lapels. Add beads to each petal tip and attach the trim to the jacket with hidden stitches.

The sleeves, clasp, and jacket back have additional motifs formed from a bowtie pair of tent leaves and a yo-yo circle center that is completely covered with beads. The contrasting stitching on the jacket was disguised with narrow black cording that was hand couched in place over the stitching. A row of black beads was added for sparkle.

RIGHT: Black trim was couched in place on this customized backpack. Tent leaves (page 79) for both the flowers and leaves were each made with 2" of 1" wide (#5) black wire-edged ribbon. The flowers have beaded centers and the leaves a single bead at their join. The quilted crosshatching is embellished with a bead at the intersections. A zipper fob of black trim is attached to the zipper.

TOP RIGHT: A tapestry jewelry box takes on new life with a diagonal arrangement with a gathered rose (page 64), signature rose (pages 73–74), petaled rose buds (page 76), and gathered leaves (page 83). Lace and buttons complete the embelllishments.

LEFT: Make reversible snowflakes from white ribbons in a variety of sizes and textures, both soft and wire-edged. Cut the ribbon length twice the width of the ribbon. Form six tent leaves (page 79), sew together, and gather up tightly to form the snowflake. Cover the centers of both sides with accents of buttons, beads, or pearls. Add a cord and you are ready to decorate the tree.

BELOW: Different widths and textures of white and silver metallic ribbons were used to form leaves for this winter wonderland garland. Tent leaves (page 79) and a gathered leaf (page 83) of sheer organdy wired ribbon form the three-leaf units for the garland. The tip of one of the largest leaves in each unit was accented with pearls.

TOP LEFT: A purple suede jewelry case topped with a pair of beautiful silk gathered roses (page 64) on a base of lace provides just the right amount of contrast for this mini-bouquet. Accent with gathered leaves (page 83) and a shirred ruffle of silk to complete the look. A lavender filled organdy pillow becomes a lovely garden pillow when accented with a cluster of pansies (page 46).

TOP RIGHT: Ordinary ballpoint stick pens become fun to use when you turn them into flowers. Glue three velvet leaves to the top and add one signature rose (pages 73–74). Wrap the pens with ribbon for stems.

RIGHT: These fobs are made from an assortment of mini flowers, leaves, and buds and are accented with beads. You won't be able to stop making these delightful little treasures. Use these floral fobs on your cell phone, scissors, zipper pulls, or make a mobile of fobs. Hang from a bulletin board for a floral accent. Gold cording provides a loop for attaching.

TOP LEFT: Turn a favorite mug into a sewing kit. A padded foam core top is made using wool batting and covered with velvet. A quarter silk rose using 9" of ribbon (page 75) and a pair of rosebuds made the same way using 6" of ribbon are nestled in a pair of checkered ribbon leaves (page 83). A fifth leaf is folded over to hide all the raw edges. Use a hot glue gun to attach the velvet cover. Add a 15"–18" length of silk cording to one edge of the cover and tie to the handle. On the opposite edge, add a little arrangement of leaves, rosebuds, and cording to form a handle. Store sewing supplies inside the mug.

TOP RIGHT: The brim of this straw hatlet is garnished with pleated checked black-and-white ribbon and black cording tied in the back. A fluffy bright red poppy (page 40) is made from sheer organdy and taffeta unwired ribbon. Fill the center with fluffy black yarn and finish up with two pairs of tent leaves (page 79).

BOTTOM LEFT: Customize purchased travel slippers with signature roses (pages 73–74) and checkered green tent leaves (page 79). The silk rose is crush-proof and travels beautifully.

Straight-Stitch Flowers

The straight-stitch technique is an easy method that makes a wonderful variety of flowers. Gather the ribbon tightly or loosely, depending on the look you want to achieve. In instances when you want the gathers very close to the selvage and you are using wire-edged ribbon, you can make your gathers without stitching a single stitch by carefully sliding the ribbon along its wire.

Simple Posies

1

2

The size of the flower is determined by the width of ribbon you use.

For each flower, you need:
    2" length of ¾" wide (#3) ribbon *OR*
    2" length of 1" wide (#5) ribbon (as in the
        photo) *OR*
    3" length of 1½" wide (#9) ribbon

3–4

1. Begin ½" from the cut edge. Using doubled, knotted thread stitch a row of running stitches through the center length of the ribbon, ending ½" from the cut edge.

2. Gather the ribbon as tightly as possible and secure the gathers with a few backstitches.

3. Fold over the raw end edges to form a circle. Secure the ends together with hidden stitches on a crinoline square base.

4. Add a bead or French knot in the center.

Variations: Use novelty ribbon for many beautiful varieties of posies. Vary the stitching distance from the center of the ribbon to closer to the selvage edge. This will produce a bell-shaped flower with a narrow edge of gathers on one side of the stitching and wide gathers on the other side.

Calendulas

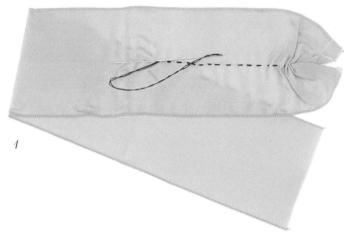

For each flower, you need:

12" of 1½" wide (#9) wire-edged ribbon

9" of 1" wide (#9) ribbon *OR*

6" of ¾" wide (#3) ribbon

1. Begin ¼" from the cut edge. Using doubled, knotted thread, stitch a running stitch through the center length of the ribbon. Every few inches, gently pull the thread and gather the ribbon.

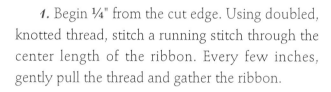

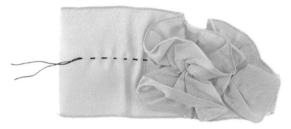

2. When you have stitched to the end of the ribbon and gathered the ribbon fairly tightly, secure the gathers with a few backstitches. Cut the thread.

3. Tuck the cut edges of the ribbon ends underneath the flower and tack the flower's center to the petals.

4. Anchor the flower to your background fabric with a few hidden stitches through the center of the flower.

"I feel the personality of each flower, and I find myself greeting them as if they were human. 'Good morning, beloved friends! Are all things well with you? And are you tranquil and bright? And are you happy and beautiful?' They stand in their peace and purity and lift themselves to my adoring gaze as if they knew my worship, - so calm, so sweet, so delicate radiant, I lose myself in the tranquility of their happiness."

CELIA THAXTER, *AN ISLAND GARDEN*, P. 113

Bell Flowers

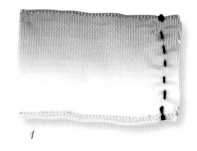

1

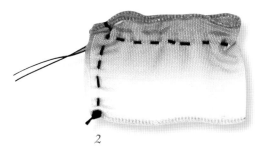

2

3

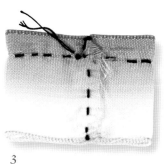

4

5

For each flower, you need:

   3" of 1" wide (#5) wire-edged ribbon

1. Fold the ribbon in half and stitch the cut ends together using a doubled, knotted thread and a running stitch ¼" in from the edge. Secure with a few backstitches.

2. Spread the ribbon loop open and make a running stitch ¼" from the selvage completely around the ribbon loop.

3. Gather the stitches tightly and secure the gathers with a few backstitches. Cut the thread.

4. Position the seam to the middle of the back and flatten the blossom.

5. Stitch the blossom onto the stem and add beads/stamens.

Variation: Make blossoms by gathering the opposite edge to reverse the color placement. Roll the lower front edge up a bit and add beads for the look of stamens peeking out from the flower.

Mountain Laurel

"The jealous bees and butterflies
follow the flowers I carry also,
sometimes all the way into the house."
CELIA THAXTER, *AN ISLAND GARDEN,* P. 112

1

2

For each flower, you need:
  3½" of #3 wired ribbon

1. Remove the wire from the edge that will become the center of the flower (white edge).

2. Fold the ribbon in half.

3. Stitch the cut ends together using a doubled, knotted thread and a running stitch ¼" from the ends. Secure with a few backstitches.

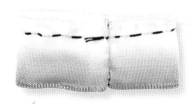

3

4. Turn the loop inside out and make a running stitch ¼" from the selvage, stitching completely around the ribbon loop.

5. Gather stitches tightly and secure the gathers with a few backstitches. Cut the thread. Open out the flower to form a circle. Mold the outer wired-edge up and toward the center to form a cup-like flowerette.

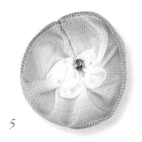

4

Make multiple flowerettes and cluster them in groups on a piece of crinoline. Secure to background fabric with several hidden stitches.

5

Wisteria

And have you seen the charming things
That have no power to speak,
The dear, sweet humble little flowers
That all so silently
Teach such a lovely lesson every day,
To you and me?
Go seek them, if you know not,
When summer comes once more
You'll find a pleasure in them
You never knew before!

THE POEMS OF CELIA THAXTER, "SEASIDE FLOWERS"

The porch on Celia's cottage was shaded with these lovely fragrant blooms. While they are a joy to behold, after 10 years, I am still waiting for my wisteria on my porch to bloom. I love this flower and thankfully can make as many glorious blooms as I wish in silk.

For each flower, you need:
   36" of 1" wide (#5) purple-to-white ombre
      wire-edged ribbon

1. Using doubled, knotted thread stitch a row of running stitches through the center length of the ribbon.

2. Gently gather the ribbon every few inches. Do not pull too tightly. The ribbon should swirl around itself as it is pulled.

3. Stitch and gather the entire length of ribbon, leaving the thread attached. Mold the ribbon into a triangular shape on a piece of crinoline. When the shape is pleasing and no gaps are visible, secure to the crinoline using hidden stitches. Add leaves to the crinoline base before trimming off the excess crinoline.

4. Attach wisteria to the background fabric through the gathered sections of ribbon and crinoline using hidden stitches.

1

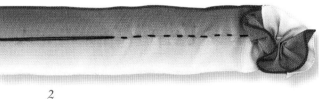

2

3

Ribbon Treasures from Celia's Garden ❀ Faye Labanaris

Carnation

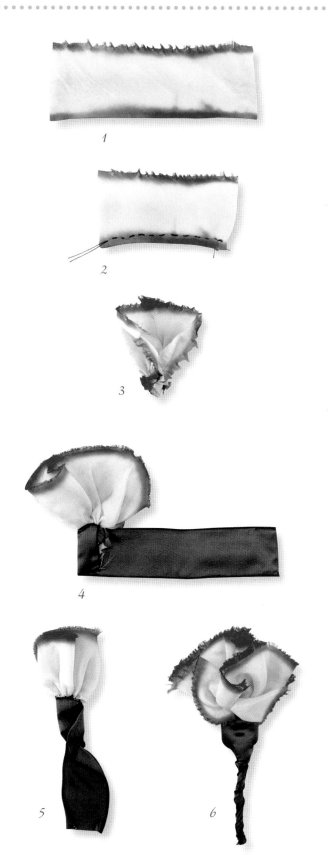

For each flower, you need:

    36" of 1" or 1½" wide bias-cut ribbon for
        carnation

    6"–9" of 1" wide (#5) green ribbon, wired
        or unwired

1. Distress the outer edge of the bias ribbon by pulling it against one blade of a pair of scissors. You can also run your thumbnail against the ribbon to produce a slightly frayed and ruffled edge.

2. Using doubled, knotted thread, stitch a row of small running stitches the length of the ribbon, close to the selvage edge.

3. Gather tightly and roll the gathered ribbon to form the flower. Stitch the raw end under and secure with a few backstitches.

4. To form the green stem base of the carnation, take the 1" wide green ribbon and wrap around stitched gathers on the base of the flower.

5. Stitch the green ribbon to the bottom of the carnation as you wrap. Go around twice forming a tightly coiled base.

6. Do not cut the ribbon. Squeeze the base of the green coil and stitch through the base to form a narrow end. If you're using wire-edged ribbon, twirl the remaining length of ribbon to form a twisted stem.

Gathered-on-Wire Flowers

This technique involves gathering ribbon on the wire in a piece of wire-edged ribbon. It saves you from having to stitch the length of ribbon by hand. It is not complicated but you have to proceed with a gentle hand at first until you get the feel of the strength of the wire. Too hard a pull will snap the wire and you'll have to finish with a needle and thread.

Hold the wire with one hand, or with a hemostat or tweezers, and gently slide the ribbon down the wire with the other hand, pulling the ribbon straight along the wire. (Pulling at an angle could cause the wire to cut the ribbon.) Don't force the ribbon to slide or you'll break the wire. Wrap the wire around the ends to secure the gathers.

Flat-Circle Poppy

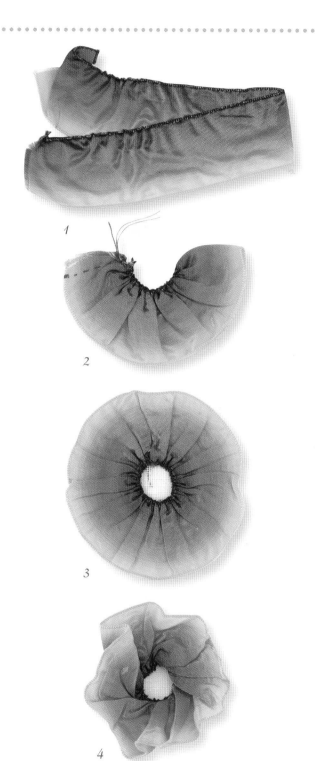

For each flower, you need:
  9" of # 5 ribbon per poppy *OR*
  12" of # 9 ribbon per poppy

1. Gently gather the ribbon on the wire as tightly as possible. Wrap the wire around itself and the a bit of ribbon to secure the gathers.

2. Seam the cut ends together.

3. Open to form a flat circle. Anchor the center of the circle onto a square of crinoline.

4. Tape the crinoline securely to a flat surface. Hold onto the edges of the ribbon and twist like you are turning a sharp corner with a steering wheel. When you like the look of the swirls, secure the edges to the crinoline with hidden stitches.

5. Fill the center opening with stamens, beads, or knotted embroidery floss.

"We usually think of a Poppy as a coarse flower, but it is the most transparent and delicate of all the blossoms of the field. The rest, nearly all of them depend on the texture of their surfaces for color. But the Poppy is painted glass; it never glows so brightly as when the sun shines through it. Whenever it is seen, against the light always it is a flame and warms the wind like a blown ruby...."

CELIA THAXTER, *An Island Garden*, P. 82

Celia's Poppies

1

2

3

For each flower, you need:
   36" of 1½" (#9) wide wire-edged red-
      orange ribbon

1. Push the cut edge of the ribbon back to expose about one inch of wire from both ends of one edge of the ribbon. Gently bend the wire back over the ribbon to keep it from sliding back.

2. Starting at one end, gently gather half the length of ribbon by sliding it down the wire. When the ribbon is half gathered fairly tightly (without forcing), secure the gathers by wrapping the wire around itself and the selvage edge. Repeat from the other end of the ribbon.

3. Form a flat circle with the gathered ribbon on crinoline, spiraling the gathered ribbon on top of itself, gradually making the center opening smaller, and pin together to hold the shape.

4. Fill the center with black embroidery floss, fringed trim and/or beads. Attach the flower to the background fabric through the flower center.

Curtain tiebacks – Poppies are made with sheer unwired ribbon. Black-and-white check ribbon tent leaves (page 79) on a backing ribbon form tiebacks.

Butterfly Orchid

For each flower, you need:
    18" of #9 white wire-edged ribbon and
    4" of #3 yellow for the flower center

1. Fold the ribbon into thirds, lengthwise, and pinch the folds for guide creases.

2. Unfold and form into a U-shape as shown. Pin the folds.

3. Snip the wire at the Xs as indicated in the photo and remove the wire from the X sections on either side of the folds.

4. Using a doubled, knotted thread, stitch a running stitch as shown.

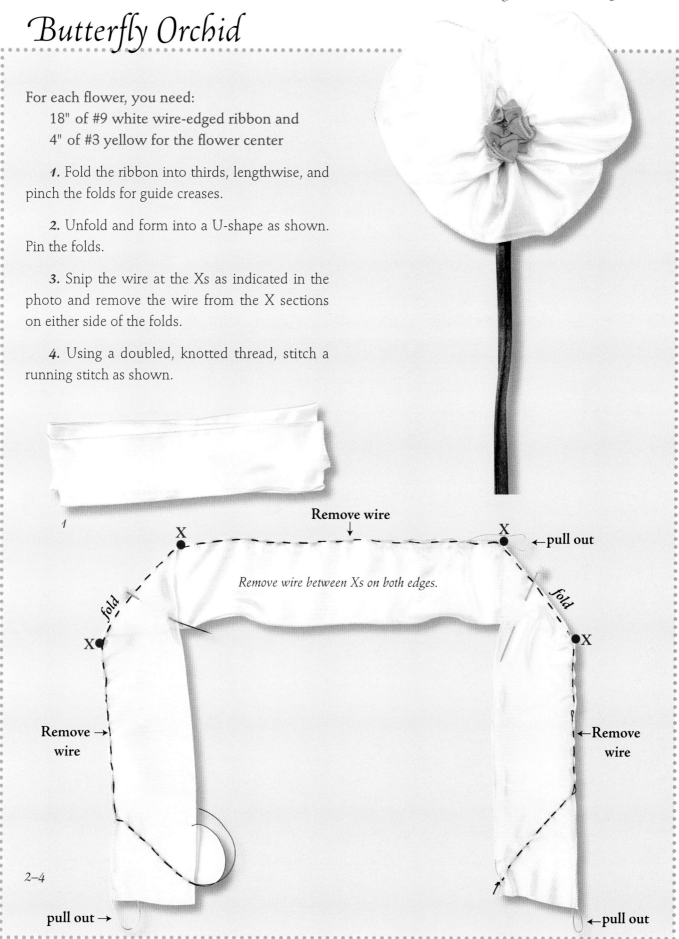

Remove wire

X ← pull out

Remove wire between Xs on both edges.

fold   fold

X   X

Remove → wire   ← Remove wire

1

2–4

pull out →   ← pull out

Butterfly Orchid *continued*

5. Gently pull the thread and gather tightly. Secure the gathers with a few backstitches.

6. Untwist and arrange the petals with the two smaller petals on top of one larger bottom petal. Gently flatten but do not join together. Trim the tails to half their length. Bring the tail ends together and pin to hold in place.

7. To form the yellow center, stitch a row of running stitches through the center length of the ribbon. Gently gather the ribbon into a puff. Secure the gathers with a few backstitches.

8. Add the yellow center to cover the cut tails and arrange the petals underneath the yellow. Secure all with hidden stitches. Arrange the two top petals into a butterfly shape.

9. Stitch a wired stem to the back for a free-standing orchid.

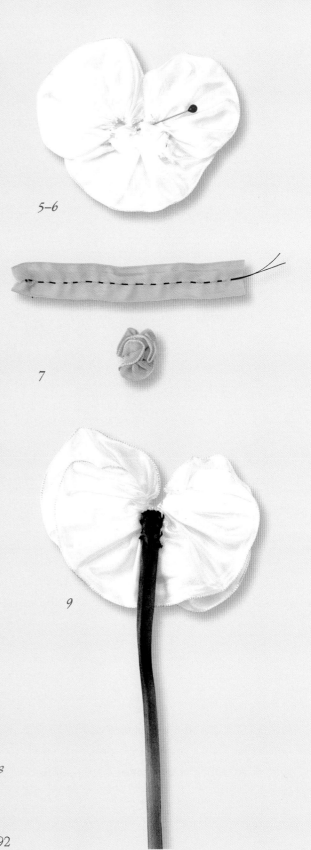

5–6

7

8

9

"As I work among my flowers, I find myself talking to them, reasoning and remaining with them, and adoring them as if they were human beings. Much laughter I provoke among friends, but that is of no consequence.

We are on such good terms, my flowers and I!"

CELIA THAXTER, *AN ISLAND GARDEN*, P. 92

Fuchsia

For each flower, you need:

4½" of 1½" wide (#9) ombre, wire-edged ribbon

1. Fold in half and pinch the wire edges to mark the center.

2. Open flat and fold the cut ends in to the center crease and pin as shown. These pins will serve as your stitching guide.

3. Use doubled, knotted matching or contrasting thread and bring up through the inside of a fold and come out at the halfway pin point. Stitch a diamond pattern through both thicknesses, looping your thread over the edge of the ribbon at each corner point in your stitching.

4. Fold a few strands of stamens together and tie them with thread or wire to hold them together. (You could substitute knotted embroidery floss for stamens.)

5. Gather the ribbon slightly and insert the cluster of stamens.

6. Finish gathering as tightly as possible and secure. Arrange the petals so that the front pair lies above the back pair. When using variegated ombre ribbon, wonderful two-tone combinations result.

Vary the blossoms by increasing the amount of ribbon used or by selecting a different width of ribbon.

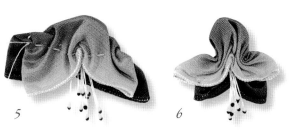

Forget-Me-Nots

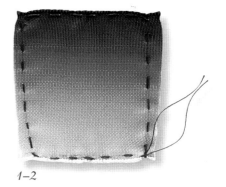

1–2

These delightful miniature four-petal blossoms are easier to make than they look. They are lots of and fun and use up small scraps of ribbon.

For each flower, you need:
1½" of 1½" wide (#9) wire-edged ribbon

1. Remove the wire from both edges of the ribbon.

2. Use doubled, knotted matching or contrasting thread and stitch a running stitch close to one selvage edge, starting and stopping ⅛" away from the cut ends. Do not cut the thread.

3. Gather the ribbon tightly.

4. Arrange to form a yo-yo.

5. Turn over to form a flat circle.

6. Bring your doubled thread up through the center, go over the edge of the ribbon and back through the center again. Tightly pull.

7. Repeat this around the circle until all the petals are formed.

8. Add a bead or pearl in the center.

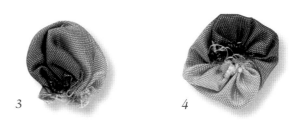

3   *4*

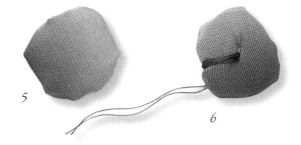

5   *6*

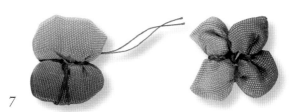

7

8

Ribbon Treasures from Celia's Garden ❀ Faye Labanaris

Violets

For each flower, you need:
  4 strips 2½" long of 1" wide (#5) wire-
    edged ribbon

1. Trim both ends at a 45° angle.

2. Using a double, knotted matching thread, stitch ½" from the cut end, across the narrow selvage edge and up the other cut end.

3. Gently pull the thread and gather the petal as tightly as it will go.

4. Secure the gathers with a few backstitches and cut the thread.

5. Repeat these steps for a total of four petals.

6. Attach the petals to themselves or a crinoline base with a few overlapping stitches to form a complete circle. Pull the center together with needle and thread. The center will be slightly open. Attach the flower to background fabric with stitches through the center.

Heavily bead the center area to camouflage all raw edges. Sculpt or fold the outer wired petals toward the center to form a turned edge.

Variation: Remove the shorter wire from each piece of ribbon for a tighter center gather. For softer petals, use unwired ribbon.

Pansies

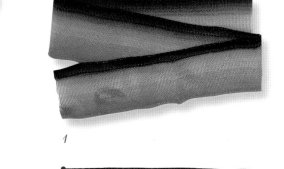

1

2–3

For each flower, you need:

two pieces, 7" and 5", of ¾" wide (#3)
wire-edged ribbon *OR*

two pieces, 12" & 6", of 1" wide (#5) wire-
edged ribbon *OR*

two pieces, 18" & 12", of 1½" wide (#9)
wire-edged ribbon

small scrap of narrow yellow ribbon for the
center

1. For the front, three-petal portion of the pansy, fold the longer piece of ribbon into thirds and pinch at the folds in the ribbon.

2. Unfold the ribbon, refold as shown, and pin the folds.

3. Snip the wire edge on either side of the folds and remove the wire from the three outside edges. Omit this step when using #3 ribbon.

4

4. With a double, knotted thread, make a running stitch as shown.

5. Gently gather the ribbon and flatten out the three petals

6. Fold in half to bring cut ends together and secure with a few back stitches through the knots.

5

6

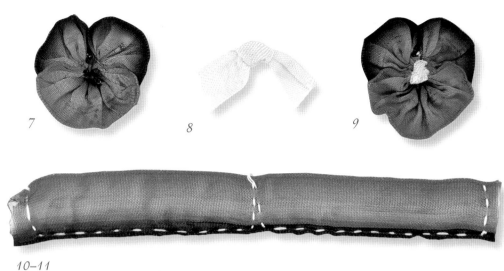

7   8   9

10–11

7. Spread the petals open so the center bottom petal lies on top of the two other petals.

8. Tie a knot in the yellow ribbon, insert it in the center, and secure to the pansy with a few backstitches.

9. Insert the yellow knot into the center of the pansy and secure with a few stitches.

10. For the back, two-petal portion of the pansy, fold the shorter piece of ribbon in half and pinch at the fold.

11. Unfold and with a doubled, knotted thread stitch two square-U patterns.

12. Gather fairly tightly.

13. Straighten out the two petals so the bottom edge is straight and the petals overlap. Stitch these two petals on a corner of a piece of crinoline.

14. Place the three-petal portion in front and on top of the two petals and secure with hidden stitches through the knot area.

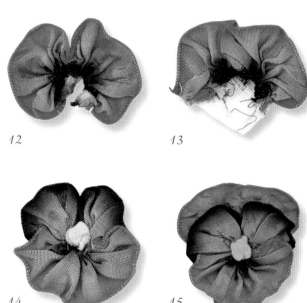

12   13

14   15

"The pansy seeds lie like grains of gold on the dark soil. I think as I look at them of the splendors of imperial purples folded within them, of their gold and blue and bronze, of all the myriad combinations of superb color in their rich velvets. Each one of these small grains means a wealth of beauty and delight."

CELIA THAXTER, *AN ISLAND GARDEN*, P. 15

Petal Variations

Flowers with pointy petals are easily made by folding ribbon, cutting ribbon from templates, or making loops. Use these methods to grow a bouquet of daisies, starflowers, and daffodils.

Daisies, Sunflowers & Starflowers

For each petal, you need:

    a piece of ribbon twice as long as it is wide

1. Decide how many petals you want in your flower, cut and fold that many pieces of ribbon as for a tent leaf (page 71). For a starflower, make five petals.

2. Position the petals all facing the same way (wire edges up or down). With a doubled, knotted thread, string the petals together by stitching across the raw edges, picking each up as if you were holding an ice cream cone.

3. Connect the first and last petal and gently gather to form a circle—tightly for a daisy or starflower and loosely for a sunflower. Secure with a few backstitches. Attach the circle of petals to a piece of crinoline and anchor the through the inside edge.

4. Make a ribbon button center for the daisy or a fabric center (right) for the sunflower. Stitch around a circle of fabric to form a yo-yo. Lightly stuff with a little batting for a puffed center.

Starflower Variation: To make the petals, use 7½" of #9 ribbon; cut five 1½" squares. Take a square of ribbon, folded twice on the diagonal. Add a padded center (page 85).

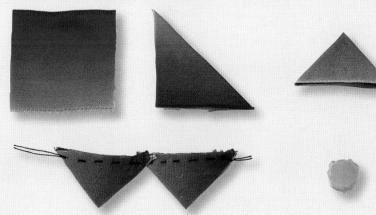

Autumn Flower Variation: Use plaid ribbon and follow the directions on page 48. Use 3" of 1½" wide wire-edged plaid ribbon. Finish with ribbon button centers on both sides to make a reversible flower.

Cut-Ribbon Pointy Petals

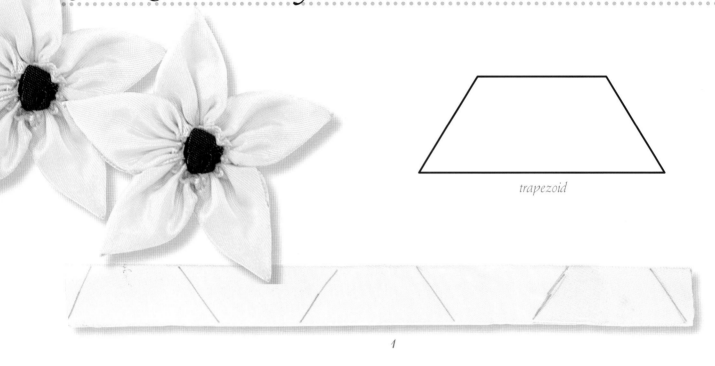

trapezoid

1

2

For each petal, you need:
    1" wide (#5) ribbon

1. Trace the trapezoid template onto template plastic and cut out.

2. Use the template to mark a length of 1" wide (#5) ribbon as shown.

3

3. Cut out the ribbon segments and fold as shown.

4. Complete the flower following steps 2–6, from page 48.

4

5. Knot a small piece of narrow ribbon for the center.

Note: If using varigated or ombre ribbon, use twice as much ribbon and get 2 sets of petals for 2 differently colored flowers.

5

Looped-Petal Daisy

For each petal, you need:

    4" of narrow ribbon, about ½" wide

    Cut 12 petals for the daisy.

1. Bring the cut ends together and overlap them to one ribbon width.

2. With a doubled, knotted thread, stitch at least two running stitches through both layers, ¼" from the cut ends.

3. Stitch all petals together and gather tightly to form the flower.

4. Add a flower center of your choice.

Variation: Tie a knot in the center of each 4" piece of ribbon for a knotted looped petal.

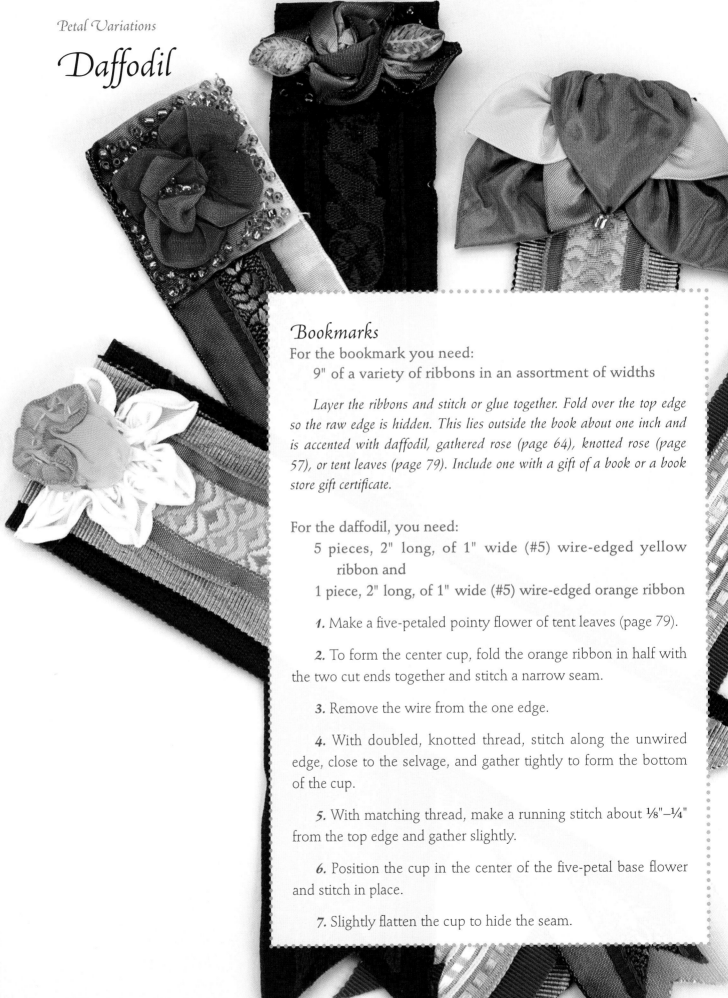

Daffodil

Bookmarks

For the bookmark you need:

   9" of a variety of ribbons in an assortment of widths

Layer the ribbons and stitch or glue together. Fold over the top edge so the raw edge is hidden. This lies outside the book about one inch and is accented with daffodil, gathered rose (page 64), knotted rose (page 57), or tent leaves (page 79). Include one with a gift of a book or a book store gift certificate.

For the daffodil, you need:

   5 pieces, 2" long, of 1" wide (#5) wire-edged yellow ribbon and

   1 piece, 2" long, of 1" wide (#5) wire-edged orange ribbon

1. Make a five-petaled pointy flower of tent leaves (page 79).

2. To form the center cup, fold the orange ribbon in half with the two cut ends together and stitch a narrow seam.

3. Remove the wire from the one edge.

4. With doubled, knotted thread, stitch along the unwired edge, close to the selvage, and gather tightly to form the bottom of the cup.

5. With matching thread, make a running stitch about ⅛"–¼" from the top edge and gather slightly.

6. Position the cup in the center of the five-petal base flower and stitch in place.

7. Slightly flatten the cup to hide the seam.

Patterns for Stitched Petals

Stitched petals are basically variations of the ruching technique (page 54). In addition to straight stitching, other patterns of running stitches can be used to make single or multiple petals, depending on the length of ribbon and how many times the stitching pattern is repeated.

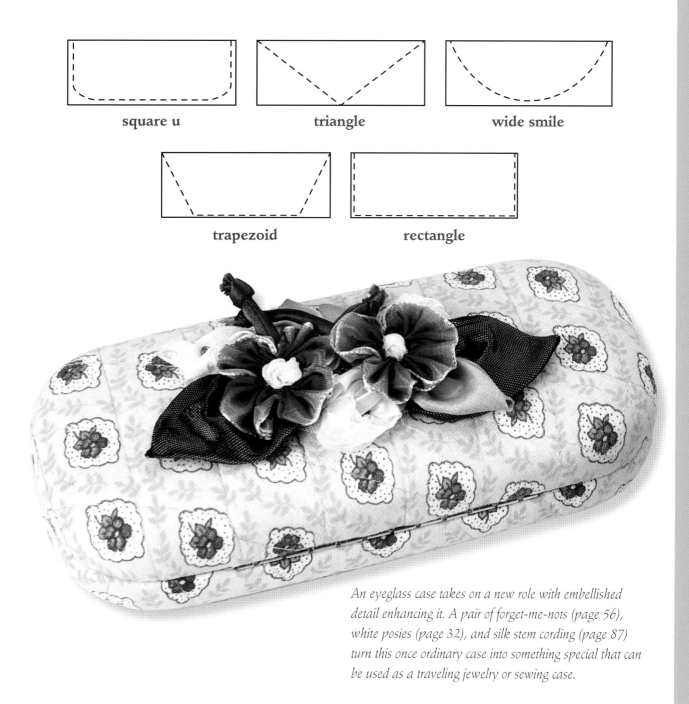

square u   triangle   wide smile

trapezoid   rectangle

An eyeglass case takes on a new role with embellished detail enhancing it. A pair of forget-me-nots (page 56), white posies (page 32), and silk stem cording (page 87) turn this once ordinary case into something special that can be used as a traveling jewelry or sewing case.

Three-Petal Flower

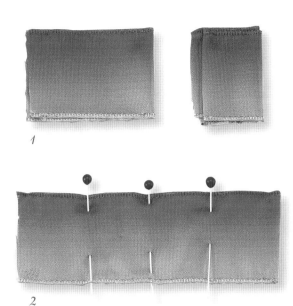

For each flower, you need:

    3" of 1" wide (#5) ribbon *OR*

    4½" of (#9) ribbon

1. Fold the ribbon in half, then almost in half again, leaving ⅛" tail at each end. Finger press the folds.

2. Open the ribbon flat and mark the folds with pins.

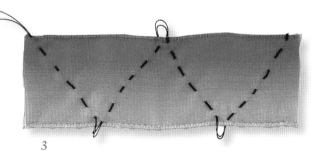

3. With doubled, knotted thread, stitch a running stitch in the triangle pattern as shown. This stitching pattern is known as ruching.

4. Gather to form a three-petal blossom, then clip excess.

5. Secure the gathers with a few backstitches.

Note: If you continue the ruching stitch on a longer length of ribbon, a multi-petaled circular flower will result.

"Like the musician, the painter, the poet, and the rest, the true lover of flowers is born, not made."

CELIA THAXTER, *AN ISLAND GARDEN*, P. 5

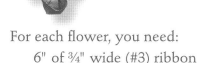

Round Petal Flower *variation*

For each flower, you need:
   6" of ¾" wide (#3) ribbon

1. Mark off five 1" spaces along ribbon, leaving a ½" tail at each end.

2. Stitch a rectangle-shaped running stitch as shown and gather for a five-petal round petal flower. Be sure to flip thread over the ribbon's top edge and come down to the bottom..

3. Gently gather the ribbon one petal at a time. When all petals are formed stitch the first and last petal before stitching the next petal. Flatten out the flower.

4. Secure the formed flower to crinoline with a few stitches. Add beads to complete the center.

Note: Vary the length of ribbon and spacing of sections and you will change the shape of the petal.

A notepad becomes a decorative accessory for your desk or phone area. Using the cover design for inspiration, I added round petal flowers, three velvet split leaves (page 80), and stems of Hannah silk cording (page 87).

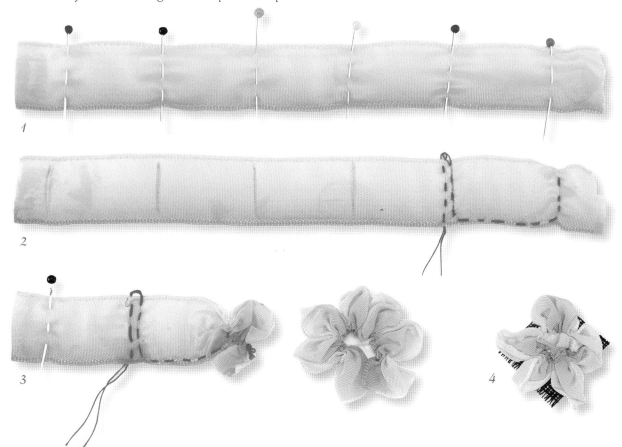

Two-Tone Three-Petal Flower

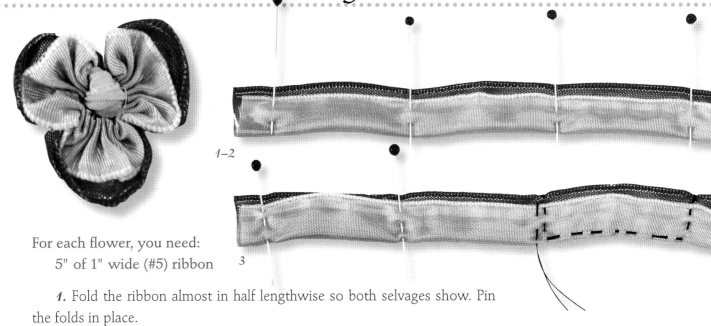

1–2

3

For each flower, you need:
5" of 1" wide (#5) ribbon

1. Fold the ribbon almost in half lengthwise so both selvages show. Pin the folds in place.

2. Mark three evenly sized spaces with pins, ¼" in from the cut edges.

3. With a doubled, knotted thread, sew a rectangle pattern of running stitches. Be sure to flip thread over the ribbon's top edge and come down to the bottom.

4. Gently gather the ribbon one petal at a time. When all 3 petals are formed flatten out the flower.

5. Fold in half to bring cut ends together and secure with a few back stitches.

6. Knot a small piece of yellow ribbon for the flower center. Insert and secure with a few backstitches.

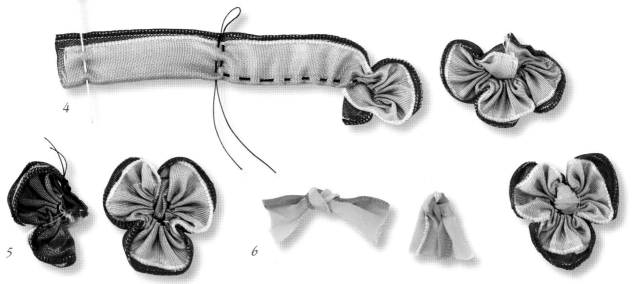

4

5

6

Multi-Petaled Roses

Constructing the Rose Center

Start by making the center of the rose to provide an anchoring base for sewing on the petals. Make your rose center with dark or light ribbon to contrast with the petals.

Form the center of each rose using one of these techniques:

Knotted: Tie a length of ribbon into a loose knot and trim, leaving a 1" tail on either side of the knot.

Twirled: Fold a piece of ribbon in half lengthwise. Make a diagonal fold at the end of a length of ribbon and twirl the ribbon, encasing the fold. When the twirl is as full as desired, trim the ribbon, leaving a 1" tail. Secure with a few backstitches.

Crimped: Gather a 6"–12" length of ribbon and tightly roll. Secure with a few backstitches. If using wire-edged ribbon, scrunch down the top edges to form a convoluted center with lots of irregular folds.

Variations: Form a center with a bunch of stamens OR combine the stamens with one of the center techniques descried above. Enhance the center with beads either stitched singly or in loops. Add a fringe of embroidery floss.

Ruched Rose Petal Techniques

Stitched petals are basically variations of the ruching technique, which has been around for over 150 years. Ruching is accomplished with running stitches done in a repeated pattern and then gathered. Ruching is varied by the stitching pattern itself, the length of the repeats, and the width of the ribbon being ruched.

Rose Petals

There are six basic techniques for making rose petals. They are numbered here for easy reference when following the "rose recipes" (pages 67–72).

- #1 Simple U-stitched
- #2 Rolled-top edge
- #3 Flat single diagonal-rolled corner
- #4 Folded ribbon with two diagonal-rolled corners
- #5 Folded ribbon with pinched corners
- #6 Gathered on wire

When doing any gathering or ruching, be sure to use a doubled strong thread so that the thread will not break as you're pulling up the petals. Always flip the thread over the ribbon's selvage edge when changing direction, taking the next stitch by coming in from the back. This will allow the thread to slide like a pulley when it is being gathered so it will not bunch up, knot, and break.

Begin with a 3"–4" length of 1½" wide (#9) ribbon for each petal. With wire-edged ribbon, you can shape or sculpt the petals. If you use unwired ribbon, you will have to add a few extra stitches to hold the folds and rolls in place.

Once you have mastered the six basic petal techniques, experiment with different lengths and widths of ribbon for different looks. Any of the petals can be used by themselves to form a rose or you can build your rose using combinations of the various petals. (See the Rose Recipes, pages 67–72.)

Technique #1: *Simple U-Stitched Petals*

A single layer of ribbon is used for this petal and the length can vary. These petals work best for the outer rows of your rose as they look like a petal that has opened completely.

For each petal, you need:
3"–4" of 1½" wide (#9) ribbon

1. With a doubled, knotted thread, stitch three sides in the Square-U pattern.

2. Gently pull the thread to gather the ribbon into a pleasing petal shape.

3. Secure the gathers with a few backstitches.

Optional: If using wire-edged ribbon, remove the wire from the stitched bottom edge for a tighter gather.

1

2–3

"The 'sweet and cunning hand of Nature' is so lavish of its work, and it is all so happy, the joy is so exhaustible, the refreshment to the human soul is heavenly!"

CELIA THAXTER, *AN ISLAND GARDEN*, P.121

Note: 4"–6" lengths of ribbon are used for the u-stitched petals in these roses.

Technique #2: *Rolled-Top Edge*

For each petal, you need:
   3"–4" of 1½" wide (#9) ribbon

1. Tightly roll the top edge of the length of the ribbon by winding it around a round wooden toothpick several times.

2. Remove the toothpick and pin the rolls to hold in place.

3. With a doubled, knotted thread stitch three sides in the Square-U pattern.

4. Remove the pins and gather fairly tightly.

5. Secure the gathers with a few backstitches.

This petal tends to cup inward and should be placed to face the center of the flower. The outer rolled portion of the petal faces away from the center.

Use this petal between the tightly rolled center petals and the full outer petals. Three of these petals and a knotted center will form a beautiful cabochon rose that can also be used by itself or as the center of a rose.

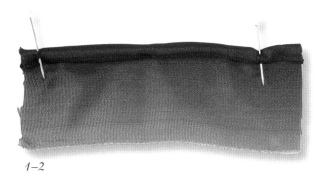

1–2

3

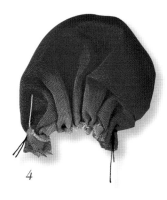

4

5

Technique #3: *Flat Single Diagonal-Rolled Corner*

For each petal, you need:
   3"–4" of 1½" wide (#9) ribbon

1. Tightly roll one corner of the ribbon around a round wooden toothpick on the diagonal, ending the roll when one edge touches the bottom of the ribbon. Remove the toothpick. Pin the rolled edge to hold in place.

2. With a doubled, knotted thread and starting at the roll, stitch a running stitch along the selvage and up along the cut end ¼" from the edge.

3. Remove the pin and pull the thread to form a straight line and gently gather to form a petal. Secure the gathers with a few backstitches.

4. Push the gathered edge inward to form a cupped petal with the roll to the outer edge.

Variations: Gently squeeze the top rolls into a pointed petal.

If using ombre ribbon, vary the position of the rolls on either the light side or the dark side for two different effects from the same ribbon.

1

2

3

4

Technique #4: *Folded Ribbon with Two Diagonal-Rolled Corners*

For each petal, you need:
  3"–4" of 1½" wide (#9) ribbon

1. Fold the ribbon in half.

2. Using a round wooden toothpick, start at a folded corner and roll the ribbon tightly toward the center of the fold.

3. Roll the other side to mirror the first roll and slightly overlap the rolls at the tip.

4. With doubled, knotted thread, stitch a running stitch at the cut ends through both thicknesses and gently gather to form a petal OR pinch pleat an anchor with a stitch in the center of the bottom edge.

Variation: Leave a space between the rolls for a more unfurled looking petal.

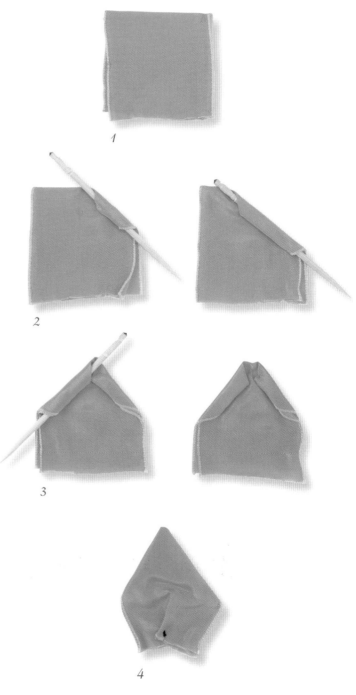

Note: All leaves for this rose are made with the same petal technique.

Technique #5: *Folded Ribbon with Pinched Corners*

For each petal, you need:
   3"–4" of 1½" wide (#9) wire-edged ribbon

1. Fold the ribbon in half and pinch the edges to mark the center.

2. Open and refold lengthwise. Stitch the ribbon together at the pinched points with a few backstitches.

3. Spread the ribbon open and fold in half, bringing the two cut edges together.

4. With doubled, knotted thread, make a pinch pleat in the center of the lower edge through both thicknesses OR make a running stitch and gather gently. Secure the pleat or gathers with a few backstitches.

5. The flower center is knotted trim anchored to crinoline.

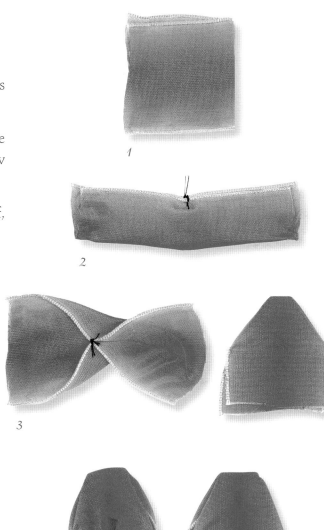

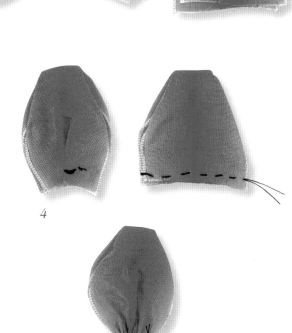

Technique #6: *Gathered on Wire*

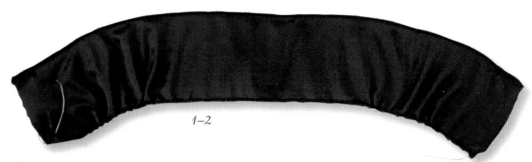

1–2

For each petal, you need:
   12"–18" of 1½" wide (#9) wire-edged ribbon

1. Push the ribbon back from the wire and wrap it around the cut end of the ribbon.

2. Push the ribbon back from the same wire at the other end of the ribbon and grip the wire with a hemostat or tweezers.

3. Gently push the ribbon along the wire to form gathers.

4. Wrap the wire around the ribbon to secure the gathers.

3

4

Variations: Use this technique with a shorter length of ribbon to make a rose center. Tightly roll the gathered ribbon around itself. Pinch in the top folds to form a crimped center.

Make a present even more special by giving it in a simple drawstring gift bag. Choose an elegant fabric and enhance it with a gathered rose.

Ribbon Treasures *from Celia's Garden* ❀ Faye Labanaris

Constructing a Multi-Petaled Rose

Sew individual petals around the center of the rose in an arrangement of concentric circles.

Overlap the petals in the innermost row by about half the width of the petals and gradually decrease the overlap on subsequent rows until the petals are butting up next to each other in the outermost row. Use long straight pins to hold the petals in place as you stitch to secure them to the rose center and to each other.

Row 1 – overlap about ½ with 3 petals

Row 2 – overlap about ¼ with 5 petals

Row 3 – petals butt next to each other, 5 plus petals

Start with three petals, then five in the second row, and the same number or a few more in subsequent rows. Place so the tips of the petals in the new row fill the space between the petals in the previous row. Fold back the outer petals for an open look.

Vary the length and width of the ribbon to change the size and shape of the petals. Don't be afraid to experiment. Enhance the look of your roses by combining different shades and textures of ribbon. After adding the final row of petals, sew the rose to a backing of crinoline. The crinoline makes it easier to sew on the leaves.

Thread Sculpting Your Roses. This step is like playing hairdresser. Once you've made your rose, the next step is to fine tune its appearance. Any rose can be enhanced with this primping technique. Use hidden stitches to form tucks or gathers in the petals. Use a #10 or #11 straw /milliners needle and 50- or 60- weight fine thread in a matching color. Mount the rose on crinoline as a base for lots of anchoring stitches before the rose is placed on a background fabric with just a few stitches.

"Near my own seat in a sofa corner at one of the south windows stands yet another small table, covered with a snow-white linen cloth embroidered in silk as white and lustrous as silver. On this are gathered every day all the rarest and loveliest flowers as they blossom, that I may touch them, dwell on them, breathe their delightful fragrance and adore them. Here are kept the daintiest and most delicate of vases which best set off the flowers' loveliness."

CELIA THAXTER, *AN ISLAND GARDEN*, P. 97

Thread Sculpting

Combine Petals to Make Six Basic Rose Shapes:

Flat—This rose is the simplest of the roses and usually has five petals that surround a central area of stamens.

High-centered—This shape is most often associated with the formal hybrid tea roses. The petals rise to a point in the center.

Loosely-doubled—These roses have anywhere from five to 25 petals and their shape is of a full-blown open rose.

Quartered—This rose has an almost flat center area and is divided into four distinct sections. It is packed with an abundance of petals.

Rosette—This rose has a flat shape and is literally bursting with overlapping and unevenly spaced petals.

Urn-shaped—This rose has petals that are flat on the outside, but curve to an urn shape in the middle.

Rose Recipes

Roses can be constructed of petals all made with the same technique or made with a variety of techniques. The following rose recipes give examples of just a few of the possible combinations. These should give you a starting point for your own variations.

Song

I wore your roses yesterday:
About this light robe's folds of white,
Wherein their gathered sweetness lay,
Still clings their perfume of delight.

And all in vain the warm wind sweeps
These airy folds like vapor fine,
Among them still the odor sleeps,
And haunts me with a dream divine.
So to my heart your memory clings,
So sweet, so rich, so delicate:
Eternal summer-time it brings,
Defying all the storms of fate,

A power to turn the darkness bright,
Till life with matchless beauty glows,
Each moment touched with tender light,
And every thought of you a rose!

THE POEMS OF CELIA THAXTER, "SONG"

Center – clustered yellow stamens or knotted yellow embroidery floss

Row 1 – 3 petals #2 (rolled top edge & stitched)

Row 2 – 5 petals of #3 (flat ribbon with single diagonal rolled corner)

Row 3 – 6 or 7 petals of #4 (folded ribbon with two diagonal rolled corners)

Rose Recipes

Center – gathered ribbon
  (#6) and crushed
Row 1 – 5 petals of #3
Row 2 – 5 to 7 petals of #3
  longer length per petal

Center – knotted center
Row 1 – 3 petals of #2
Row 2 – 3 petals of #3
Row 3 – 5 petals of #4
Row 4 – 5 petals of #6

Center – hidden knot   **Row 4** – 5 petals of #4
Row 1 – 3 petals of #2   **Row 5** – 5 petals of #3
Row 2 – 5 petals of #3   **Row 6** – 7 petals of #1
Row 3 – 5 petals of #4

Center – knotted center
Row 1 – 3 petals of #2
Row 2 – 3 petals of #3
Row 3 – 3 petals of #3 with
  longer length per petal

Center – twirled center
Row 1 – 3 petals of #4
Row 2 – 3 petals of #3
Row 3 – 5 petals of #3 with
     longer length per petal

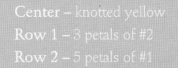

Center – knotted yellow
Row 1 – 3 petals of #2
Row 2 – 5 petals of #1

Center – rolled
Row 1 – 5 petals of #1
Row 2 – 3 petals of #1 black

Center – rolled center
Row 1 – 3 petals of #2
Row 2 – 3 petals of #3
Row 3 – 3 petals of #3
Row 4 – green / 3 petals of #1

Rose Recipes

Center – gathered #6 and crushed
Row 1 – 3 petals of #2
Row 2 – 6 petals of #4
Row 3 – 3 tent leaves of split velvet

Center – knotted
Row 1 – 3 petals of #2
Row 2 – 3 petals of #3
Row 3 – leaves: 4–5 petals of #4

Center – gathered #6
Row 1 – 3 petals of #6 satin
Row 2 – 6 petals of #1
Row 3 – 3 petals of #3

Center – knotted
Row 1 – 3 petals of #2
Row 2 – 5 petals of #3
Leaves – 3 of #4

Center – clustered stamens
Row 1 – gathered rose #6 and
swirled
Row 2 – 4 petals of #3
Row 3 – 3 petals of #2

Center – tightly gathered and crushed #6
Row 1 – 3 petals of #2
Row 2 – 5 petals of #3
Row 3 – 6 or 7 petals of #3 longer length
per petal
Row 4 – 9 petals of #4

Center – crimped (See page 57.)
Row 1 – 3 petals of #3
Row 2 – 5 petals of #3

Center – #6 tightly gathered and crushed
Row 1 – 3 petals of #3
Row 2 – 4–5 petals of #3
Row 3 & 4 – #6 gathered with various
lengths, colors, and textures of ribbon

Rose Recipes

Center – knotted
Row 1 – 3 petals of #3
Row 2 – 4–5 petals of #2
Row 3 – 5 petals of #3

Center – knotted
Row 1 – 3 petals of #3
Row 2 – 5 petals of #3 with
longer length per petal

Center – knotted
Row 1 – 3 petals of #1 with slightly
crushed edges
Row 2 – 3 petals of #3
Row 3 – 5 petals of #3
Row 4 – 8–9 petals of #4

Center – knotted
Row 1 – 3 petals of #1 crinkled edges
Row 2 – 5 petals of #3
Row 3 – 5 petals of #3
Row 4 – 5 petals of #1 with longer
length of sheer ribbon per petal

Favorites from My Rose Garden

My Signature Rose

This is probably the easiest of all the roses to make and one of my favorites. It is the rose I wear most often.

For each rose, you need:

    36"–45" 2½" wide silk satin bias ribbon

    18" 1½" wide silk bias ribbon for leaves

1. Fold the ribbon in half lengthwise. Pin to hold the first few inches of the fold in place.

2. Fold down a 2" section at the right-hand end of the ribbon at a 45° angle.

3. Fold the diagonal fold over to meet the straight fold. Repeat the fold.

4. With a doubled, knotted thread, secure the three folds with a few anchoring stitches going through all the layers.

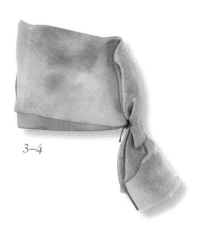

5. Twirl the folded portion along a short length of the ribbon to form the center of the rose. The amount of twirl is up to you. When it looks right, anchor the twirl in place with a few more stitches. Cut the thread and reknot it.

continued

My Signature Rose *continued*

6. Bring the needle up through the fold at the opposite end of the ribbon from the twirled center and anchor the thread with a few backstitches. Sew a running stitch along the cut end and along the selvage edges ¼" from the edge through both thicknesses, stitching all the way to the twirled center.

7. Gently gather the ribbon to about 6" in length. Roll the gathers around the twirled center. If you gather the ribbon too tightly, you'll have a rolled ruffle. If you gather too loosely, your rose will droop. You can always unroll the ribbon and adjust the gathers until you're happy with the look of your rose.

8. Secure the gathers by stitching each layer to the previous layer.

9. Fold an 18" length of green ribbon to form a looped bow. Tie in the center and place behind rose.

10. Fasten the rose to a piece of felt or Ultrasuede® fabric and add a pin to the back.

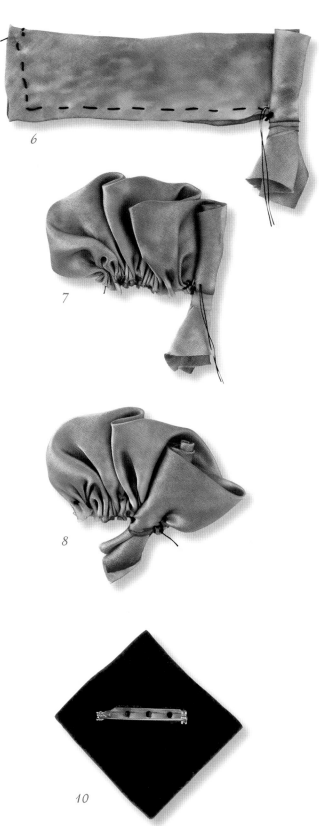

6

7

8

9

10

Quarter Roses

For each petal, you need:
   3"–4" of 1½" wide (#9) ribbon OR
   2"–3" of 1" wide (#5) ribbon

1. Make five petals with technique #4, folded ribbon with two diagonal-rolled corners (page 62).

2. Arrange the cupped petals around a tightly twirled center to form a "just opening" rose.

3. Stitch the petals together at the base and insert into a simple green calyx of ribbon, fabric, or Ultrasuede fabric or wrap green ribbon around the petals to form a base.

Mini bouquets or tussy mussies were made by Celia Thaxter from her garden of flowers. She gave these as special gifts each day. Now you can do the same thing by making flowers into bouquet pins.

In Memorium
(To Celia Thaxter)

Oh where dwells my lady of Long Ago
   Whose garden was out at sea?
Each year when the lilies and larkspur grow
   She appears again to me.
We laid her to rest to the sea's dirge song
   Deep down in her island tomb...
Has she slept there still with the dead so long
   Bound fast in their land of gloom?
No! Her radiant spirit dwells not there,
   But in sunlight realms above...
In all the gardens, and everywhere.
   She abides with light and love.

MARY LIVINGSTON TARLETON

MAY 1911

Rosebuds

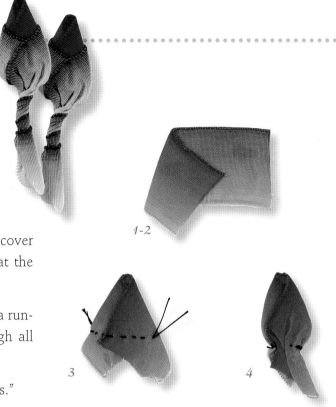

For each rosebud, you need:
    1½" of ¾" wide (#3) ribbon *OR*
    2" of 1" wide (#5) ribbon *OR*
    3" of 1½" wide (#9) ribbon and
    a piece of green ribbon for the calyx

1. Fold down one end to form a triangle.

2. Fold the other portion of ribbon to cover this fold, leaving a small gap in the folds at the tip. Pin in place.

3. With a doubled, knotted thread, take a running stitch across the bottom edge through all layers.

4. Pull the thread and "gather ye rosebuds."

1-2

3

4

Rosebud *variation*

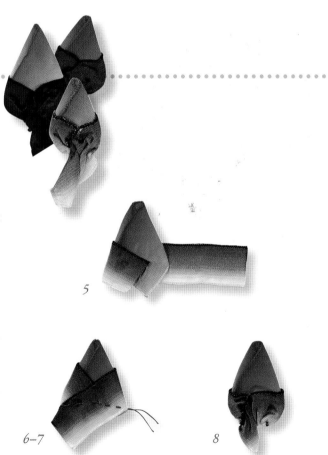

After step 4, above, wrap the green ribbon as follows:

5. Place the flat rosebud on a 3" piece of ¾" wide (#3) ribbon 1" from the left edge.

6. Fold the left end down over the rosebud at a sharp angle. Fold the right-hand length down in the same manner, forming a deep V.

7. With a double, knotted thread, take a stitch at the V through all the layers. Travel the thread from the back to the lower corner of the green ribbon and backstitch.

8. Make a running stitch across the bottom through all the layers, and gather tightly. Secure the gathers with a few backstitches.

5

6–7

8

Two-Tone Rosebuds

For each rosebud, you need:
3" of 1½" wide (#9) ombre or variegated
ribbon with green as one of the colors

1. Fold the ribbon not quite in half lengthwise so the color on both edges shows.

2. Position the ribbon so the shorter fold is facing down.

3. Fold the ribbon into thirds to form a triangle.

4. With doubled, knotted thread take a running stitch across the bottom through all the layers, and gather tightly.

5. Secure the gathers with a few backstitches.

6. Cluster for an interesting effect.

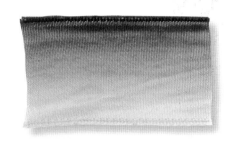

1

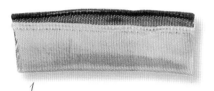

2

3

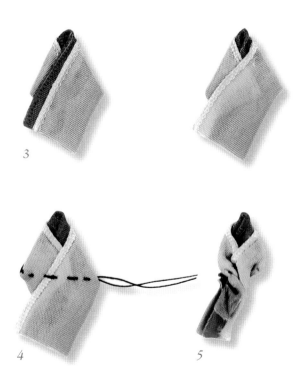

4   5

Leaves, Stems & Berries

Flowers need leaves and stems to complement them. Using a variety of green ribbons, fabrics, and trims will give a richness to your floral creations. Ribbon leaves can be stitched and flattened for a subtle effect or left dimensional for a realistic effect. Fabric leaves can be appliquéd flat or seamed and turned for a dimensional fabric leaf. Make stems flat or with cording (page 88). Save your green ribbon and fabric scraps for making leaves and stems. Use beads for embellishment or cluster them to form berries.

Fabric Leaves

Fabric leaves can be made in a variety of ways.

Cut leaf shapes from a variety of shades of green fabrics, adding a turn-under seam allowance to appliqué. Alternatively, sew two leaf shapes, wrong sides together, using two different fabrics for the top and back of the leaf. Turn right sides out.

Cut Ultrasuede® leaves to the exact size and shape desired. Appliqué in place.

Draw veins with a permanent fabric pen or embroider them with matching or contrasting thread, either by hand or machine.

Add interest to appliquéd leaves by embroidering around the outer edge with an outline, stem, or chain stitch with matching or contrasting thread.

Cut leaves whole from a printed leaf fabric.

Cut a leaf of Ultrasuede and finely clip the edges for a rough-edged leaf.

Treat ribbon as fabric and cut a leaf to appliqué.

Use fabric to make tent leaves (page 79), folding down a ¼" of fabric along the top edge before folding into the tent-leaf shape.

Tent Leaves or Pointy Petals

This versatile, easy-to-make shape makes beautiful leaves as well as floral petals simply by selecting a blossom-colored ribbon instead of green. These can be used smooth-side up or vein-side up, depending on the effect you want.

For each leaf or petal, you need:

A piece of ribbon twice the length of the ribbon's width (2:1 proportion, *for example:* 1" wide = 2" cut length)

1. Fold the ribbon in half and pinch the edge to mark the center point.

2. Unfold the ribbon to lie flat.

3. Fold the left half of the ribbon down at a 45° angle so the cut edge lies just below the selvage opposite the pinched center point.

4. Repeat with the right half. The folds should form a "tent" or prairie point shape.

5. Pin through the center to hold the edges together.

Stitch a row of running stitches along the bottom edge with a doubled, knotted thread, through all the layers of ribbon.

6. Gather to the desired shape.

7. Secure the gathers with a few backstitches.

If you are using wired ribbon, remove the bottom wire for a tighter gather.

Vary the size of the leaf or petal by varying the width and length of the ribbon used.

1–3

4–5

6–7

"He who is born with a silver spoon in his mouth is generally considered a fortunate person, but his good fortune is small compared to that of the happy mortal who enters this world with a passion for flowers in his soul.

CELIA THAXTER, *AN ISLAND GARDEN*, P. 4

Fabric Tent Leaf *Variation with a Folded Edge*

1. Cut a strip of fabric about ¼"–½" wider than the 2:1 proportion for a piece of ribbon.

2. Fold over ¼"–½" along one side and press.

3. Proceed as you would for a ribbon tent leaf. Take a tiny tack stitch at the tip to hold the point in place.

1–2

3

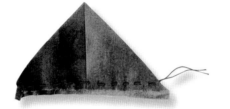

Split Leaf *with* Velvet *and* Satin

Use this technique for any ribbon that has two distinct sides.

For each leaf, you need:
> a piece of ribbon slightly longer than twice its width

1. Fold one end of the ribbon down toward you at a 45° angle.

2. Fold the second end down away from you to expose the opposite side.

3. Pin to hold in place.

4. Stitch across the bottom edge catching all the layers.

5. Remove the pin and gently gather to form a two-tone leaf. Secure the gathers with back stitches.

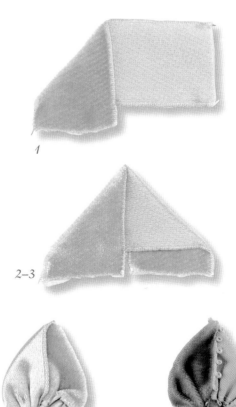

1

2–3

4–5

Pointy Tip, Long Leaves

For each leaf, you need:

3" of 1½" wide (#9) wire-edged ribbon

1. Fold in half lengthwise. Using doubled, knotted thread, stitch a seam on one end. (This step may be done on the sewing machine if you need lots of leaves in a hurry.)

2. Turn the stitched end inside-out and flatten it into a triangular shape. The wire will allow the triangular tip to hold its shape.

3. Using doubled, knotted thread, stitch a row of running stitches on the remaining cut end.

4. Gather tightly and secure with backstitches.

This technique works with any width ribbon. If using unwired ribbon, finger press or iron the point and anchor the leaf to its background fabric with additional stitches.

Variation: Make both ends of the ribbon into pointy tips and gathered in the center. This bowtie leaf which can be twisted to form a pair of leaves.

Like the tent leaves, these leaves can be used to make flower petals simply by selecting blossom-colored ribbons.

1

2

3   4

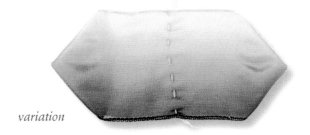

variation

"Of course it goes without saying that climbing vines should not be set where there is nothing upon which they may climb. Indeed that would be simple cruelty - nothing more or less."

CELIA THAXTER, *AN ISLAND GARDEN*, P. 70

Mitered Leaves *from Flat Ribbon*

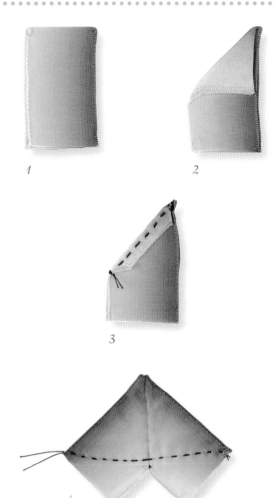

1

2

3

4

5

This leaf can be made with different widths of ribbon, either wired or unwired.

For each leaf, you need:
   3" of 1" wide (#5) ribbon *OR*
   4" 1½" wide (#9) ribbon

1. Fold the ribbon in half and finger press along the fold.

2. Fold the center fold down at a 45° angle.

3. Stitch across the angled fold and trim the excess ribbon about ¼" away from the folded edge.

4. Unfold the ribbon and stitch a running stitch across the bottom as shown.

5. Gently gather to form the leaf.

If you use a variegated ribbon, making the 45° angle fold in the opposite direction will give you an opposite colored leaf.

A porcelain pin is enhanced with a variety of tent leaves, ribbon blossoms, and beaded blackberries and raspberries.

Gathered-Ribbon Leaves

For each leaf, you need:
  4"–6" ¾" wide (#3) ribbon

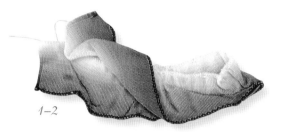

1–2

1. Fold the ribbon in half, bringing the cut ends together.

2. Push on the two cut ends of ribbon to expose the wire on one selvage edge .

3. Using a pair of tweezers or a hemostat to hold the two wires, slide the ribbon along the wire, gathering the ribbon on the wire fairly tightly.

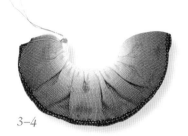

3–4

4. Secure the gathers by wrapping the wires around one end of the cut edges.

5. Whipstitch the gathered center edges together either on top of the wire edge or below the wire for two distinct center veins.

5

6. Spread the ribbon open to form a gathered leaf. Cover the raw bottom edge by tucking it under a flower or another leaf.

7. For a finished edge leaf, completely wrap the cut ends of the ribbon with the wire, then tuck the wrap under the opened leaf.

6

8. Gathering the opposite edge of the variegated ribbon gives the leaf a different appearance.

For a heart-shaped or ivy leaf, slide the gathers down toward the base of the leaf before whipstitching the gathered edges together.

Variations: This can be used as a flower petal by using ribbon with flower colors. This technique makes a very large leaf when made with #5 or #9 ribbon.

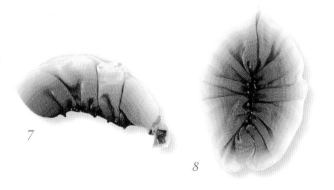

7

8

Holly Leaf Variation

For each leaf, you need:

    6" of ¾" wide (#3) ribbon

1. Follow the Gathered Ribbon Leaves instructions(page 83).

2. Pinch the wire edges into holly leaf points with your finger tips or a hemostat.

3. Stitch the leaf onto crinoline, easing in the pointy edges as you go.

4. Accent with a cluster of 3 holly berries (page 85).

Holly leaves, berries, and Faye's signature rose are used for a Christmas garland to enhance your holiday decor.

Holly Berries *or Padded Flower Center*

For each berry, you need:
   1½" of 1½" wide (#9) ribbon
   If using wire-edged ribbon, remove the wire from both edges.

1. With doubled, knotted thread, stitch a tiny running stitch completely around the perimeter of the ribbon, taking care to stitch about ⅛" away from the cut edges and very close to the woven selvage edge.

2. Gather tightly and flatten to form a yo-yo. Secure the gathers with back stitches, then bring your thread through the yo-yo, coming out at the folded edge. Secure with a few back stitches.

3. Holding the folded edge of the yo-yo between your thumb and fingers, stitch a tiny running stitch around the perimeter through just the top edge of the fold, taking care to stitch through just one layer of fabric.

4. Place your thumb and finger over the center "bellybutton" and gently gather until the ribbon begins to curl around the tip of your thumb.

5. Remove your thumb and gather as tightly as possible and secure with back stitches to complete the berry.

Cluster two or three holly leaves together and secure three berries on top of the leaves. Use to embellish a holiday quilt or a wreath wallhanging, use as a holiday ornament, or wear as a pin.

Variation: This can be used as a padded flower center.

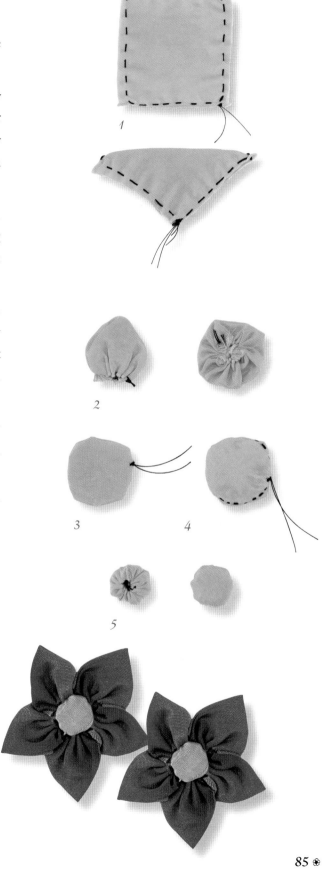

Boat or Lily Leaves

These leaves are made from a piece of ribbon that is folded and stitched, resulting in a center-gathered leaf with pointy tips at both ends. If a striped ribbon is used, an interesting color pattern results. If an ombre or two-tone ribbon is used, then a split-color leaf results.

These leaves are fun to make and are great for using up scraps of ribbon. You can vary the amount of ribbon used. You can use any type of ribbon for this leaf also. This leaf can easily become a flower petal with a different color of ribbon.

For each leaf, you need:
    1½" of ¾" wide (#3) ribbon OR
    2" of 1" wide (#5) ribbon OR
    3" of 1½" wide (#9) ribbon
    Use ombre ribbon for a two-tone leaf.

1. Fold in half lengthwise, then fold the ends up away from the bottom fold at a 45°angle. Pin to hold in place.

2. With a doubled, knotted thread, stitch a running stitch along all three folded edges.

3. Gently gather the ribbon until the stitching forms a straight line. Secure the gathers with back stitches. Trim the folded ends to ¼".

4. Fold the ribbon open and pinch the tip into a point.

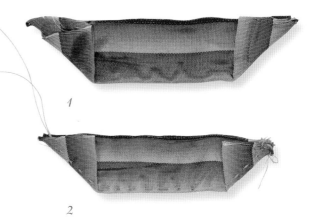

1

2

3

4

Welcome, a thousand times welcome,
   Ye dear and delicate neighbors—
   Bird and bee and butterfly, and
     Hummingbird fairy fine!
   Proud am I to offer you a field
     For your graceful labors.
   All the honey and all the seeds are
     Yours in this garden of mine.

And the world is full of perfume
   And color and beautiful motion,
   And each new hour of this sweet
   Day the happiest seems and best.
   THE POEMS OF CELIA THAXTER, "GUESTS"

Wired Stem

For each stem, you need:
    Hannah bias silk cording and
    18 gauge wire cut to the length desired
        for the stem

1. Hold the cord, push the silk back, and snip off about 1" of the cording.

2. Tie a knot in the trimmed end of the silk.

3. Cut the knotted length of about 1" longer than your wire length.

4. Slip the wire into the cording tube.

5. Trim 1" of cotton cord from the open end.

6. Position the silk-wired stem behind your flower and turn the raw edges of the silk under. Stitch securely to the flower. Bend your stem to the desired shape.

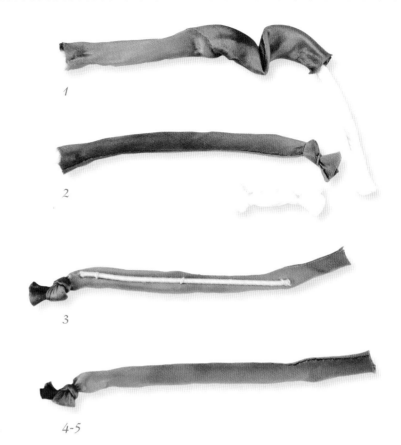

1

2

3

4-5

"I have no words to tell you what pleasant work this is!"

Celia Thaxter, *An Island Garden*, p. 48

6

Use stemmed poppies for a favorite vase, for a favorite spot on your desk, or on a window sill.

Stems

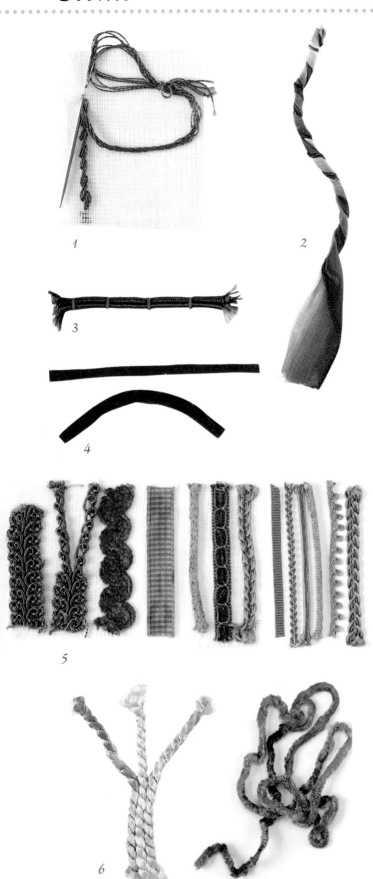

1

2

3

4

5

6

1. Embroidered stems. The embroidery can be done by hand or machine. If by hand use an outline or chain stitch. If using a machine, a narrow satin stitch works nicely. With the many threads available, don't hesitate to combine them for a new look.

2. Twisted ribbon. Narrow #3 size wire-edge ribbon can be tightly twisted to form a stem. It can be bent into any shape and couched down into place on your background fabric.

3. Couched stems. Couching involves laying down a thicker thread, yarn, or cord and anchoring it in position with a thinner thread in a matching or contrasting color. An easy way to work with cording is to glue it into place first and then stitch.

4. Ultrasuede. Cut a narrow strip of Ultrasuede® fabric for a stem in any shape and width you want. The raw edge is just stitched down and you are done.

5. Trims. Trims add interest and texture to your stems. There are so many wonderful trims and cords available. Draw your stem line on your background fabric with a pencil. Make a thin glue line on the drawn stem using a toothpick and a drop of glue. Place the trim in place and press. After the glue dries, stitch down with a few tacking stitches from behind.

6. Yarn and cording. In addition to trims, you can use yarn and cording. If the yarn or cording chosen is too thin, just twist several lengths together for a twisted "cord" and couch down into position. Use a thin glue line as a holding medium. If you try to stitch down without the glue, the stem tends to wander and will not lie straight.

Beaded Berries

Make realistic blackberries and raspberries by stitching beads onto crinoline. Choose black or reddish beads.

For the berries, you need:
   4 mm. round beads

1. Anchor a double, knotted matching thread to crinoline with a few small backstitches.

2. Pick up one bead and stitch it onto the crinoline.

3. Add beads around the center bead, forming a flat circle.

4. Stitch more beads onto the circle of beads, heaping them up and taking care to fill all the gaps.

5. Cut the crinoline about ¼" beyond the stitched edge. Fold the crinoline over and over onto the back of the bead-work until a small square is formed. Secure with a few stitches. Add a few more beads if spaces appear. Now the berry is ready to be sewn anywhere!

Basket of Blackberries

For a basket of blackberries, you need:
   7 beaded berries
   5 tent leaves (page 71) made with 1" wide
      (#5) ribbon
   3" piece of 1½" wide (#9) ribbon

1. Fold the ribbon in half, lengthwise, tuck in the cut ends, and stitch onto a piece of crinoline by using a piece folded in half.

2. Add the tent leaves and heap on the beaded berries.

3. Anchor the leaves and berries to the crinoline with hidden stitches.

Strawberries

For each strawberry, you need:
  2½" piece of 1" wide (#5) red or ombre red ribbon
  3" piece of ¾" wide (#3) green ribbon

1. Fold ⅓ of the red ribbon down at a sharp angle.

2. Fold the remaining portion of ribbon over the first folded section, forming a sharp point at the tip of the triangle.

3. Place the folded ribbon 1" from the left cut end of the green ribbon.

4. Fold the left portion of the ribbon down over the strawberry at a sharp angle. Pin to hold in place.

5. Fold the right portion of the ribbon over and anchor with a stitch in the center of the V formed by the green ribbon. Do not cut your thread.

6. Travel the thread inside the folds back down to the lower corner of the green ribbon. Take a few backstitches, then stitch a running stitch across the base, catching all layers.

7. Pull tightly to form a leafy section over the strawberry. Twist the tails of green ribbon to form a stem. Embroider French knots on the berry.

"It is a great temptation to linger over the loveliness of every flower that unfolds, but I spare my patient readers, and leave them to pursue these fascinating researches for themselves."

CELIA THAXTER, *AN ISLAND GARDEN*, P. 121

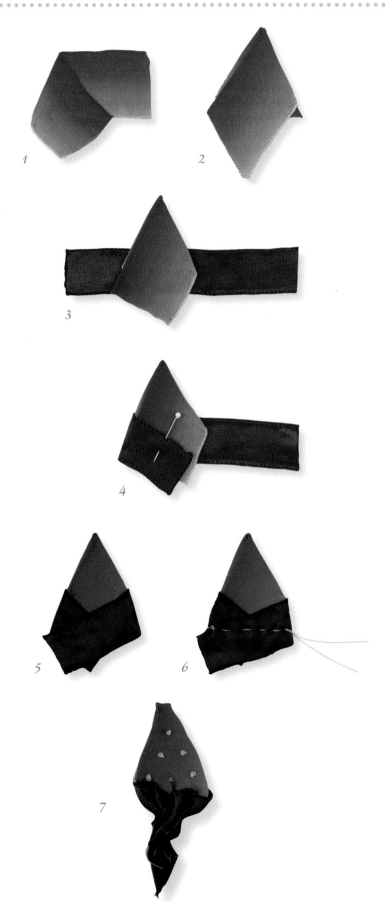

Basket of Strawberries

For the basket of berries, you need:

    3½" piece of 1½" wide (#9) ribbon for the basket

    6 strawberries (page 90)

    assorted gathered leaves (page 83) and tent leaves (page 79) of ¾" wide (#3) ribbon

1. Fold in the ends of the basket ribbon to forma basket shape and sew onto crinoline.

2. Add the assorted leaves and heap on the berries with their points facing upward.

3. Secure by stitching to the crinoline.

Footnotes

Footnotes for Celia's Story, pages 7–14

1.   Thaxter, *Among the Isles of Shoals,* 133.
2.   Ibid., 129.
3.   Thaxter, *Letters of Celia Thaxter,* 24.
4.   Ibid., 1.
5.   Thaxter, *An Island Garden,* 12.
6.   Ibid., 94.
7.   Ibid., 7.
8.   Laighton, *Ninety Years at the Isles of Shoals,* 139.
9.   Thaxter, *The Poems of Celia Thaxter,* vi–viii.
10. Thaxter, *Letters of Celia Thaxter,* 220.

Accent a garland with gathered poppies (page 40) for a casual look. They're made from an assortment of unwired #9 red ribbon with black fluffy yarn centers. The poppies are stitched on each end of wired silk corded stem so they can be freely arranged throughout the leafy garland of tent leaves (page 79).

Faye Labanaris ❀ **Ribbon Treasures** *from Celia's Garden*

Resources

FAYE LABANARIS
80 Mt. Vernon Street
Dover, NH 03820-2726
Workshops and lectures
Phone: 603 742-0211
www.fayelabanaris.com
fayequilt@comcast.net

FLOWER GARDEN RIBBONS
Project kits, ribbons, and support sup-plies available from the author. For books related to Celia Thaxter and the Isles of Shoals, contact Faye through her Web site.

Ribbon, supplies, & ribbon books

QUILTER'S FANCY
P. O. Box 457
Cortland OH 44410
800-484-7944 code 7673
www.quiltersfancy.com
orders@quiltersfancy.com
French wire-edge ribbon. Resource for wholesale or retail.

HANNAH SILK
c/o Artemis Exquisite Hannah
    Silk Embellishments
5155 Myrtle Avenue
Eureka, CA 95503
888-233-5187
www.artemisinc.com
artemissilk@aol.com

HELEN GIBB DESIGN INC.
1002 Turnberry Circle
Louisville, CO 80027
303-673-0949
www.helengibb.com
helen@helengibb.com

M & J TRIMMING
1008 6th Ave
New York, NY 10018
800-9MJ-TRIM
www.mjtrim.com
info@mjtrim.com

THE RIBBON STUDIO
13 Railroad Avenue
PO Box 944
Wolfeboro, NH 03894
603-569-9600
www.theribbonstudio.com
customerservice@theribbon-studio.com

TINSEL TRADING COMPANY
1 West 37th St.
New York, NY 10018
212-354-1242
www.tinseltrading.com
sales@tinseltrading.com

Hand-Painted Fabric

SKYDYES
Hand-painted fabric & workshops
83 Richmond Lane
West Hartford, CT 06137
www.skydyes.com
fabrics@skydyes.com

Thread and Silk Ribbon

SUPERIOR THREADS
87 East 2580 South
St. George, Utah 84790
800-499-1777
www.superiorthreads.com

Ribbon Wholesale only:

BREWER QUILTING & SEWING SUPPLIES
Formerly Quilters' Resource, Inc.
3702 Prairie Lake Court
Aurora, Il 60504
630-820-5695
www.brewersewing.com

MAY ARTS
1154 E. Putnam Ave.
Riverside, CT 06878
www.mayarts.com

RENAISSANCE RIBBONS
PO Box 699
Oregon House, CA 95962
877-422-6601
www.renaissanceribbons.com

Travel Information

To visit Celia's garden on
Appledore Island, contact:
Shoals Marine Laboratory
G-14, Cornell University
Ithaca, NY 14853
607-254-2900

To visit Star Island, Isles of
Shoals, contact:
Island Cruises, Inc.
Rye Harbor State Marina
Rte 1-A Ocean Blvd.
PO Box 66
Rye, NH 03870
603-964-6446

Bibliography

Bardwell, John D. *The Isles of Shoals A Visual History*. Portsmouth, NH: Peter E. Randall Publisher, 1989.

Curry, David Park. *Childe Hassam An Island Garden Revisited*. New York: Denver Art Museum in association with W. W Norton & Company, 1990.

Faxon, Susan C. *A Stern and Lovely Scene: A Visual History of the Isles of Shoals*. Durham, NH: University Art Galleries, University of New Hampshire, 1978.

Fields, Annie. *Authors and Friends*. Boston and New York: Houghton, Mifflin and Company, 1893, 1896.

Jenness, John Scribner. *The Isles of Shoals An Historical Sketch*. Boston: Houghton Mifflin and Company, 1884.

Laighton, Oscar. *Ninety Years at the Isles of Shoals*. Boston: The Beacon Press, Inc., 1930.

Mason, Caleb. *The Isles of Shoals Remembered A Legacy from America's Musician and Artists' Colony*. Boston: Charles E. Tuttle Company, Inc. 1992.

Parloa, Maria. *The Appledore Cook Book Containing Practical Recipes of Plain and Rich Cooking*. Boston, MA: Andrew F. Graves, 1880.

Randall, Peter. *Out on the Shoals*. Portsmouth, NH: Peter E. Randall Publisher, 1995.

Roman, Judith A. *Annie Adams Fields – The Spirit of Charles Street*. Bloomington & Indianapolis: Indiana University Press, 1990.

Rutledge, Lyman V. *The Isles of Shoals in Lore and Legend*. Boston, MA: The Star Island Corporation, 1965.

_____. *Ten Miles Out Guide Book to the Isles of Shoals*, Portsmouth, N.H. Boston, MA: Isles of Shoals Association, 1984.

Sterns, Frank Preston. *Sketches From Concord and Appledore*. New York: G. P. Putnam's Sons, 1895.

Thaxter, Celia. *Among the Isles of Shoals*. Boston: James R. Osgood & Co, 1873. Reissued. Portsmouth, NH: Peter Randall E. Randall Publisher, 1994.

_____. *The Heavenly Guest with Other Unpublished Writings*. Edited by Oscar Laighton. Andover, MA: Smith & Coutts Co. Printers, 1935.

_____. *An Island Garden*. Boston: Houghton, Mifflin and Company, 1894, 1988.

_____. *Letters of Celia Thaxter, Edited by Her Friends Annie Fields and Rose Lambs*. Boston and New York: Houghton, Mifflin and Company, 1895.

_____. *The Poems of Celia Thaxter*. Boston: Houghton, Mifflin and Company, 1896, 1899. Portsmouth, NH: Peter E. Randall Publisher, 1996.

_____. *Stories and Poems for Children*. Boston: Houghton, Mifflin and Company, 1895.

Thaxter, Rosamond. *Sandpiper – The Life and Letters of Celia Thaxter and Her Home on the Isles of Shoals – Her Family, Friends & Favorite Poems*. Francestown, NH: Marshall Jones Company, 1963.

Vallier, Jane E. *Poet on Demand – The Life, Letters and Works of Celia Thaxter*. Portsmouth, NH: Peter E. Randall Publisher, 1982, 1994.

Wheeler, Candance. *Content in a Garden*. Boston, MA: Houghton, Mifflin & Co., 1901.

Whittaker, Robert H. *Land of Lost Content: The Piscataqua River Basin and the Isles of Shoals. The People. Their Dream. Their History*. Alan Sutton Publishing Inc., Dover, NH 1993.

About the Author

I first learned about Celia Thaxter through her book *An Island Garden,* which I received as a gift from a dear friend. Celia made me feel most welcome in her garden and it was through her love of flowers that I got to know this remarkable and ageless woman. Little did I realize at that time how much of an influence she would have on my work and my life.

As a quilt teacher and lover of hand appliqué and Baltimore Album quilts, I had decided that I would make a quilt for C&T Publishing's Baltimore Album Revival Contest as soon as I read the categories and rules in the fall of 1992. I officially began thinking about the design of the quilt on January 1, 1993. I started a small sketchbook journal that day and noted in it the general quilt plan and potential blocks. I liked working with blocks set on point, so I decided upon a five-block set. The background fabric would be hand-dyed sky fabric, which is a favorite of mine. There would be an intense border of Celia's flowers.

In December 1992, I purchased an early edition of *Letters from Celia Thaxter* at an antique book store in Portsmouth, New Hampshire. When I opened the front cover I found a photograph of Celia's cottage and garden glued to the inside. On the inside of the back cover, I found something that took my breath away. There lovingly placed were dried bay leaves picked from Celia's grave on the first anniversary of her death. This was a special book. As I read about her life and her poetry, blocks began to almost design themselves. I had a feeling then that this quilt would almost make itself. The quilt was an intense journey of creation and I enjoyed every minute making it. It was a first-place winner in the Baltimore Album Revival contest and was also considered for the 20th Century's 100 Best Quilts. The quilt become the inspiration for my first book, *Blossoms by the Sea,* published by AQS. It tells the story of Celia's life and includes the blocks and flowers in the quilt.

A few years later, Celia's garden and love of flowers, along with my love of flowers and working with beautiful ribbons, combined to inspire me to create this new endeavor—*Ribbon Treasures from Celia's Garden.* I hope the reader of this book takes pleasure in working with ribbon to create beautiful flowers and to use them for special projects, gifts, and tokens of affection.

LEFT: *A TRIBUTE TO CELIA THAXTER (1835–1894), 70" x70", 1994. Faye Samaras Labanaris*

Other AQS Books

This is only a small selection of the books available from the American Quilter's Society. AQS books are known worldwide for timely topics, clear writing, beautiful color photos, and accurate illustrations and patterns. The following books are available from your local bookseller, quilt shop, or public library.

#6797   us$22.95

#7494   us$21.95

#7607   us$26.95

#7602   us$26.95

#7605   us$24.95

#5845   us$21.95

#7609   us$19.95

#7486   us$22.95

#7013   us$24.95

Look for these books nationally.
Call or **Visit** our Web site at

1-800-626-5420
www.AmericanQuilter.com